Mr. Yemi Adesina is the visionary CEO of Pristine Integrated Farm Resources Ltd, a non-profit organization dedicated to empowering youth and rural communities while combating poverty through education in Africa.

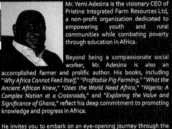

Beyond being a compassionate social worker, Mr. Adesina is also an accomplished farmer and prolific author. His books, including "Why Africa Cannot Feed Itself," "Profitable Pig Farming," "What the Ancient African Knew," "Does the World Need Africa," "Nigeria: A Complex Nation at a Crossroads," and "Exploring the Value and Significance of Ghana," reflect his deep commitment to promoting knowledge and progress in Africa.

He invites you to embark on an eye-opening journey through the captivating pages of "KENYA: A VALUABLE CONTRIBUTOR TO THE GLOBAL STAGE." In this groundbreaking book, you will unveil the vibrant tapestry of Kenya's global impact, exploring its immense contributions that resonate worldwide.

Immerse yourself in the awe-inspiring cultural heritage, breathtaking landscapes, and vibrant traditions that define Kenya. From the iconic Maasai Mara to the bustling city of Nairobi, this book celebrates the Kenyan people's unique identity and enduring resilience.

Discover the inspiring stories of visionary Kenyan entrepreneurs who have revolutionized industries, fostered innovation, and elevated Kenya's presence on the global business map. Witness the transformative endeavours of change-makers dedicated to uplifting communities, promoting sustainable development, and leaving a positive legacy on the world.

YEMI ADESINA ▪ KENYA: A VALUABLE CONTRIBUTOR TO THE GLOBAL STAGE

KENYA
A VALUABLE CONTRIBUTOR
TO THE GLOBAL STAGE

Yemi Adesina

Mr. Yemi Adesina is the visionary CEO of Pristine Integrated Farm Resources Ltd, a non-profit organization dedicated to empowering youth and rural communities while combating poverty through education in Africa.

Beyond being a compassionate social worker, Mr. Adesina is also an accomplished farmer and prolific author. His books, including *"Why Africa Cannot Feed Itself," "Profitable Pig Farming," "What the Ancient African Knew," "Does the World Need Africa," "Nigeria: A Complex Nation at a Crossroads,"* and *"Exploring the Value and Significance of Ghana,"* reflect his deep commitment to promoting knowledge and progress in Africa.

He invites you to embark on an eye-opening journey through the captivating pages of *"KENYA: A VALUABLE CONTRIBUTOR TO THE GLOBAL STAGE."* In this groundbreaking book, you will unveil the vibrant tapestry of Kenya's global impact, exploring its immense contributions that resonate worldwide.
Immerse yourself in the awe-inspiring cultural heritage, breathtaking landscapes, and vibrant traditions that define Kenya. From the iconic Maasai Mara to the bustling city of Nairobi, this book celebrates the Kenyan people's unique identity and enduring resilience.

Discover the inspiring stories of visionary Kenyan entrepreneurs who have revolutionized industries, fostered innovation, and elevated Kenya's presence on the global business map. Witness the transformative endeavours of change-makers dedicated to uplifting communities, promoting sustainable development, and leaving a positive legacy on the world.

YEMI ADESINA • KENYA: A VALUABLE CONTRIBUTOR TO THE GLOBAL STAGE

KENYA
A VALUABLE CONTRIBUTOR TO THE GLOBAL STAGE

Yemi Adesina

KENYA: A VALUABLE CONTRIBUTOR TO THE GLOBAL STAGE

DOES THE WORLD NEED KENYA

YEMI ADESINA

APOLOGIA

There are bound to be – only a few, I hope – errors and omissions, and I apologise in advance. No man knows it all, especially me! And you learn more as you get older. One good thing that comes with age is that you are happy to confess what you don't know and pass the inquiry on to a specialist who probably does.

This book is dedicated to hardworking, patient, enthusiastic, generally under-rewarded, and underappreciated people of Africa, those at home and in the diaspora, and everyone interested in the welfare of the continent of Africa.

CONTENTS

ACKNOWLEDGMENTS

Although one man has written this book, it wouldn't have been possible without the many people who have been so inspirational and whose research and hard work were helpful during its writing.

I thank God Almighty for His grace to research and put my findings into a book.

I also owe much to the many people who have encouraged me to follow my dream. In particular, my late dad, Mr Solomon Olajide Adesina. And to Bola, my wife of 27 years of marriage. I thank her immensely for her undying love, support, and encouragement, which allowed me to travel, research, and practise farming in Africa for many years.

For my two sons, Femi and Seun, whose input as the second-generation African diaspora in the United Kingdom makes the book more relevant to younger Africans. I want to thank them for our lengthy chats and the healthy debates that lasted late into the night and early mornings to gather their perspectives on specific topics. I firmly believe their generation and those following beyond will move Africa further into the future.

Many people influenced me to start learning about Africa. Some of them I have met in person, and some I know through their teachings, lectures, training, research books and journals. Coming from all walks of life, the variety of sources, expertise and professions assisted me in approaching the issue from different perspectives, adding much value to this book.

My inspirations were Pastor Matthew Ashimolowo, the late Dr Myles Munro, Dr Mensah Otabil, and Bishop Tudor Bismark. These pastors spent a lot of time teaching and believing Africa could improve.

I am greatly indebted to Dr Toyin Falola, an African historian, Dr Howard Nicholas, an economist and researcher at Erasmus University Rotterdam, and Jeffrey D. Sachs et al. for their input on the impact of geography. I am further indebted to Quoras.com, Walter Rodney *for How Europe Underdeveloped Africa*. Finally, I thank Yemi Adeyemi, the founder of ThinkAfrica.net.

THE AUTHOR

Mr Yemi Adesina is the founder of Boyd Agro-Allied Ltd, one of the largest pig farms in Nigeria. He is also the CEO of Pristine Integrated Farm Resources Ltd, a non-profit organisation registered in Africa to promote youth and rural empowerment, alleviate poverty in Africa through education, and improve the productivity and livelihood of farmers from subsistence to commercial farming in Africa.

He is a qualified social worker, a seasoned farmer, and a prolific trainer. He posted 150 videos on YouTube (papayemo1) covering pig farming and African History. Over 2.5 million viewers watched the videos in over 36 countries, making it one of the most-watched videos on YouTube from an African perspective.

He is the author of *"Why Africa Cannot Feed Itself and the Way Forward"*, *"Profitable Pig Farming: A Step-by-Step Guide to Commercial Pig Farming from an African Perspective"*, *"What the Ancient African Knew"*, *"Does the World Need Africa"*, *Nigeria: A Complex Nation at a Crossroads in Africa and the World"*, and "The Unsettled Debt: Examining the Responsibility of the World towards the Democratic Republic of Congo".

Mr Yemi, a diaspora, emigrated to the United Kingdom in 1991. He studied and worked for 20 years, earning his Master's Degree in Business Administration and a Master's in Social Work in the United Kingdom. In 2010, he emigrated to Nigeria to contribute to Nigeria's food production.

QUOTES FROM PRESIDENT RUTO

"Africa being our being in debt is not by default. The current Financial system set up Africans to be in debt. The colonial masters structured African countries to transfer their wealth to them even after independence, all in the name of servicing bad debt. If you are paying eight times more in debt interest, the chances of you being saddled with debt are eight times higher than the next person."

"Our position in Africa is as follows. Let us convert our next ten years of debt repayment into a new loan. Preferably a 50-year loan with a 20-year grace period so that you .... don't have a problem with your shareholders because you haven't given away any money. You've just changed the structure. In return, we get both liquidities, and we get it urgently, and we can develop our countries. For Kenya, for example. We pay $10 billion every year to service our debt. It would make a huge difference if I had $10 billion yearly for development in Kenya instead of paying debt. ..... I will make that money available for roads for health, for water for education. It will make a hell lot of difference. We will have done something with this conference".

"We need a financial transaction tax at the global level where even countries like Kenya do not want anything for free. We want another organisation of equals where you have as much say because you pay as much as

*we do because we also pay; that's the organisation we are looking for. ...
and those resources are controlled not by IMF and World Bank because
the West have the final say in those institutions, and we, Africa, don't
have any say. We want another organisation of equals where you have as
much say because you pay as much as we do because we also pay; that's
the organisation we seek. We need a new financial architecture where
governance and power are not on a few people's hands".*

"Let's look for half a 500 billion new money. But if we distribute it the
way we did SDR, we will have nothing with SDR; Africa ended up with
$33 billion a continent of 1.2 billion people, while Europe, with 450
million people, ended up with over $150 billion, thirteen times more than
Africa ...because the was the whole architecture of the financial system
was designed. Still, it is grossly unfair when you are looking at fairness."

"The World Bank and IMF were created in three weeks following the
destruction of Europe during World War 2. .... why is it difficult for us?
Are we saying the crisis that we are going through .... is not serious
enough for us to agree on a global financing mechanism that sought out
climate change as a problem affecting all of us? Are we saying that since
1945, we have become stupid or less human?"

"The United Nations that we celebrate today was a conversation by 50
countries in two months because it was necessary, and some leaders have
the capacity to make decisions. Are we saying that we are incapable of
making the decisions that are required of us as leaders in the context of
where we are today? So I expect that we will agree in Paris and conclude
in Nairobi in three months."

FOREWORD

Kenya, located in East Africa, is significant to Africa and the world. With its diverse landscapes, abundant natural resources, rich cultural traditions, and vibrant people, Kenya uniquely shapes the future of Africa and the world.

Throughout history, Kenya has been a key player in African affairs, from the struggle for independence from British colonial rule to the country's ongoing efforts to promote regional integration and stability. Kenya's strategic location and abundant resources have made it a hub for trade and commerce, while its rich cultural heritage has made it a beacon for art, music, and literature.

The country has made significant strides in recent years in improving infrastructure, promoting private sector development, and investing in education and healthcare. Furthermore, Kenya has played an active role in regional and international affairs, contributing to peacekeeping missions, promoting economic integration in East Africa, and advocating for the rights of developing countries on the global stage.

Despite Kenya's many achievements, the country faces numerous challenges, including poverty, political instability, and corruption. These challenges have hindered progress and prevented the country from reaching its full potential. However, Kenya has immense growth opportunities, both economically and socially but particularly in renewable energy, agriculture, and tourism. By investing in Kenya's development and supporting its people, the country can become a model for progress in Africa and beyond.

As an African historian, I examine Kenya's geography, natural resources, people, political landscape, economic development, and regional and international affairs. I seek to provide insights into the country's potential for sustainable development and its role in global progress through a comprehensive analysis.

In this book, I also aim to comprehensively analyse Kenya's past, present, and future by examining Kenya's unique history and culture and its contemporary challenges and opportunities and to contribute to a greater understanding of the country's importance to the world, its potential for sustainable growth, and the challenges and opportunities ahead.

As the world faces pressing challenges such as climate change, poverty, and inequality, the role of countries like Kenya in promoting sustainable development and global cooperation has never been more important.

This book is intended for a broad audience, including students, scholars, policymakers, and anyone interested in understanding Kenya's place in the world. This book seeks to provide a balanced and nuanced perspective on the country's potential for sustainable development.

As we grapple with the global challenges of the 21st century, it is clear that no country can tackle these issues alone. We can create a better future for all through collaboration, partnership, and shared understanding. Kenya has a critical role in this endeavour with its strategic location, diverse resources, and vibrant people.

Ultimately, this book is a call to action, a recognition of the vital role that Kenya can play in promoting progress and cooperation on a global scale. By exploring whether the world needs Kenya, I hope we can better appreciate the country's unique contributions and potential and work together to create a brighter future for all.

CHAPTER 1
INTRODUCTION

KENYA IS a country that has experienced immense change and growth over the past century. From colonialism to independence, from economic struggles to impressive growth, Kenya has emerged as a leader on the African continent. In this book, we will explore the history of Kenya, its challenges, and its successes.

Chapter 2: Early History - In this chapter, we will delve into the pre-colonial era of Kenya, including the origins of the various ethnic groups, the emergence of the Swahili culture, and the arrival of Arab and Portuguese traders. We also examine the diverse cultural and social landscape of Kenya, including the country's music, literature, and art, as well as its religious and linguistic diversity.

Chapter 3 : Environmental Challenges - Kenya is home to many ecosystems, from the Maasai Mara savannahs to the Aberdare Mountains' forests. In this chapter, we will explore Kenya's environmental challenges, including deforestation, desertification, and the threat of climate change.

Chapter 5: Colonialism and Resistance - Here, we will examine the period of British colonial rule, including the exploitation of natural resources, the forced labour of Kenyan people, and the resistance movements led by figures such as Jomo Kenyatta and Dedan Kimathi.

Chapter 6: Independence and Early Struggles - With the achievement of independence in 1963, Kenya faced new challenges, including building a new government and economy. We will explore the efforts of leaders like Jomo Kenyatta and his successor, Daniel Arap Moi, to create a stable and prosperous nation.

Chapters 7 and 8: The 1990s and Beyond - This chapter will cover the period of economic liberalisation, political reforms that began in the 1990s, and the various challenges and successes Kenya has experienced since then. We will also look at the country's current state, including the ongoing fight against corruption, the impact of climate change, and the growth of technology and innovation.

Chapters 9 and 10: Kenya in the Global Arena - Finally, we will look at Kenya's place in the world, including its relationships with other African nations, its role in international organisations such as the United Nations, and its economic ties with countries around the globe.

Conclusion: Kenya has come a long way since its pre-colonial origins, and its story is one of resilience and progress. This book explores the country's rich history, challenges, and successes, and we can be hopeful that Kenya will continue to thrive in the future.

CHAPTER 2
HISTORY AND CULTURE OF KENYA

KENYA DERIVES its name from the tallest mountain in the country, Mount Kenya. The first Christian missionary and German explorer Johann Ludwig Krapf wrote the earliest record of the name in the 19th century. It is alleged that when Krapf was travelling with the local Kamba people, he asked about the name of the mountain, and the Kikuyu who lived on the slopes of the mountain people told him it was named "Kĩĩma- Kĩĩnyaa". Krapf could not pronounce the name, so he recorded the name as "Kenya". The mountain's name was later accepted as the country's name. However, it was not widely used during the colonial period, as the country was known as the East African Protectorate then. It was renamed the Colony of Kenya in 1920 and adopted the name "Republic of Kenya" when it gained independence in 1963.

Kenya, which is officially named the Republic of Kenya, is a country in East Africa that borders Tanzania, Somalia, South Sudan, Ethiopia, and Uganda. The country's southeastern part also has a coastline along the Indian Ocean.

Kenya covers an area of 224,081 square miles and has an estimated population of 49.3 million, ranking as the world's 48th most extensive and 27th most populous country. The country is subdivided into 47 semi-autonomous counties, and each county is led by a governor who is elected by popular vote. Nairobi is Kenya's capital and largest city, with an estimated population of 3.1 million people.

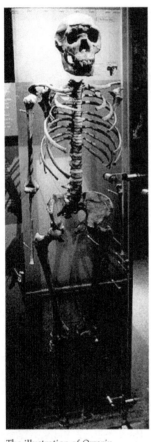

The illustration of *Orrorin tugenensis*

Kenya is one of the earliest regions where modern humans (homo sapiens) are believed to have lived. In 1929, the first evidence of the presence of ancient early human ancestors in Kenya was discovered when Louis Leakey unearthed one million-year-old Acheulian handaxes in southwest Kenya. In 2011, 3.2-million-year-old stone tools were discovered near Lake Turkana - the oldest stone tools found anywhere in the world; they pre-date the emergence of homo sapiens. One of the most famous and complete hominid skeletons ever discovered was the 1.6-million-year-old homo erectus known as Nariokotome Boy, found in 1984 on an excavation led by Richard Leakey. Evidence found in 2018 shows the early emergence of modern behaviours about 320,000 years ago in Kenya, including long-distance trade networks (involving goods such as obsidian), the use of pigments, and the possible making of projectile points. These prove that complex and modern behaviours had already begun in Africa around the time of the emergence of homo sapiens.

The first inhabitants of present-day Kenya were hunter-gatherer groups. Evidence suggests that iron production developed in West Africa as early as 3000–2500 BCE. The ancestors of Bantu speakers migrated in waves from West/Central Africa to populate much of Eastern, Central and Southern Africa from the first millennium BC. They brought iron forging technology and novel farming techniques as they migrated and integrated with the societies they encountered.

The Bantu people introduced new farming techniques, such as slash-and-burn agriculture and irrigation farming, which used water from rivers and wells to irrigate crops. These farming techniques helped increase food production and improve the quality of life for the people in the region. They also brought new products and services, like iron tools, pottery, and textiles. Iron tools allowed for more efficient farming and building, while pottery and textiles were used for household items and clothing.

The Kikuyu people are believed to have originated from the Bantu-speaking people who migrated to the Central Highlands of Kenya. The Kikuyu people developed their language, culture, and traditions, which have been preserved to this day. Their interaction with other communities, such as the Nilotic and Cushitic people, led to new ethnic groups, such as the Maasai, who developed their unique culture, language, and traditions.

Swahili, a Bantu language with many Arabic loan words, developed as a lingua franca for trade between different peoples—a Swahili culture developed in the towns, notably in Pate, Malindi, and Mombasa. The impact of Arabic and Persian traders and immigrants on the Swahili culture remains controversial. Swahili people inhabit the Swahili coast, which is the coastal area of the Indian Ocean in Southeast Africa. The Swahili coast was historically known as Azania in the Greco-Roman era and as Zanj or Zinj in Middle Eastern, Chinese and Indian literature from the 7th to the 14th century.

By the 1st century CE, many settlements, such as those in Mombasa, Malindi, and Zanzibar began establishing trade relations with Arabs. This led ultimately to the increased economic growth of Swahili, the introduction of Islam, Arabic influences on the Swahili Bantu language, and cultural diffusion. Islam rapidly spread across Africa between 614 AD – 900 AD. From the first Hijrah (migration) of Prophet Muhammad's followers to Ethiopia, Islam spread across Eastern, Northern and Western Africa. The Swahili city-states became part of a larger trade network.

Pre-colonial Kenya

Pre-colonial Kenya was a period before the arrival of Europeans and the establishment of colonialism. During this time, like most African countries, the people of Kenya had their unique way of life, including cultural and social practices that defined their traditions and beliefs. These practices were an essential part of their daily lives, and they passed them on from generation to generation.

Cultural and social practices were significant in pre-colonial Kenya and helped shape the society's identity. At the same time, cultural practices in pre-colonial Kenya were diverse and varied from one community to another. One of the significant cultural practices was music and dance. Different communities had their traditional songs and dances performed during various occasions, such as weddings, funerals, and religious ceremonies. Music and dance were for entertainment, communication, and storytelling. People could express their emotions through music and dance and pass on their history and traditions.

Social practices in pre-colonial Kenya were also essential to the society's identity. One of the significant social practices was the community's way of organising themselves. In most communities, people lived in extended families, and they had a hierarchy of authority. The head of the family was the eldest male, and he had the final say in all family matters. The extended family was also responsible for caring for the elderly and the sick. Social practices also included traditional beliefs and customs, such as using herbs for medicinal purposes, circumcision, and marriage ceremonies.

Traditionally Maasai people were pastoralists who relied on cattle for their livelihoods, and their culture emphasised cattle ownership and herding. They also had distinctive clothing, jewellery, and hairstyles, and their traditional dances and songs were essential to their cultural identity.

The Abagusii community had a council of elders who were elected by the people and acted as the community's leaders. The council made important decisions and resolved conflicts between individuals or families.

Trade was also prevalent in pre-colonial Kenya, facilitating the exchange of goods and ideas between different ethnic groups. For example, the coastal Swahili people traded with Arab traders, which led to the introduction of Islam to the region. This cultural exchange influenced the Swahili language, music, and clothing. Agriculture was also an essential aspect of pre-colonial Kenya, with different communities cultivating various crops depending on their region's climate and soil conditions. For instance, the Kikuyu people practised terrace farming on the slopes of the Mount Kenya region, which allowed them to grow crops such as yams, beans, potatoes, and bananas.

Mombasa was one of the most significant East African city-states. It was located on the coast of the Indian Ocean and was known for its bustling port and rich cultural heritage. The city-state was a hub of trade and commerce, with merchants from all over the world coming to buy and sell goods. Kilwa was another important East African city-state. It was located south of Mombasa and was known for its well-organised government and thriving economy.

2.1 IMPORTANCE OF LEARNING DIFFERENT AFRICAN CULTURES, CUSTOMS, AND ETIQUETTE

Understanding different African cultures, customs, and etiquette is essential for successful business interactions in Intra-African trade due to the following reasons:

Cultural Sensitivity: Africa is a diverse continent with numerous distinct cultures, languages, and traditions. Each African country has its own unique customs, social norms, and business practices. By understanding and respecting these cultural differences, you demonstrate sensitivity and appreciation for the values and traditions of the countries you engage with. This enhances your ability to establish positive relationships and navigate business transactions effectively.

Relationship Building: Building strong relationships is crucial in African business cultures. Africans prioritise personal connections and trust-building before engaging in business. Understanding the customs, greetings, and social protocols of the specific African cultures you are working with helps establish rapport and trust. It demonstrates your genuine interest and commitment to building long-term partnerships, which is highly valued in many African societies.

Effective Communication: Communication styles and norms vary across African cultures. Verbal and non-verbal cues, indirect communication, and high-context communication may differ from what you are accustomed to. Understanding these nuances allows you to adapt your communication approach, use appropriate language and tone, and interpret messages accurately. This facilitates effective communication, reduces misunderstandings, and fosters productive dialogue and collaboration.

Business Etiquette: Each African country has its own business etiquette and protocols. Understanding these customs helps you navigate formalities, such as greetings, introductions, and appropriate forms of address. Adhering to local business etiquette shows respect and professionalism, leading to smoother business interactions and a positive perception of your commitment to understanding and working within the local cultural context.

Trust and Credibility: Intra-African trade often involves establishing business relationships with unfamiliar partners. Demonstrating an understanding of local customs and cultural norms helps build trust and credibility. It shows that you are committed to respecting and adapting to the business practices of the specific African country, which can enhance your reputation and increase the likelihood of successful partnerships.

Cultural Preferences and Market Insights: Understanding African cultures enables you to understand better consumer preferences, market behaviours, and trends within specific African countries. Cultural insight helps shape your products, services, and marketing strategies to align with local preferences, making your offerings more appealing and relevant to the target market. This knowledge enhances your competitive advantage in the Intra-African trade.

Overcoming Stereotypes and Biases: Cultural understanding allows you to challenge and overcome stereotypes and biases that may exist about certain African cultures. By actively seeking to understand and appreciate the richness and diversity of African cultures, you can foster a more inclusive and respectful business environment that promotes collaboration and equal opportunities.

In conclusion, understanding other African countries' cultures, customs, and etiquette is vital for successful business engagement in Intra-African trade. It facilitates effective communication, builds trust, enhances relationships, and enables you to adapt your strategies and practices to align with local expectations. Cultural understanding is a key driver for thriving in Africa's diverse and dynamic business landscape.

2.2 DIVERSE CULTURES OF KENYA

Kenya, located in East Africa, is a diverse country known for its stunning landscapes, vibrant wildlife, and, most importantly, its rich cultural heritage. With over 40 ethnic groups, each with its own unique traditions, languages, and customs, Kenya boasts a captivating tapestry of cultures that have shaped the nation's identity. This section delves into some of the prominent cultures of Kenya, highlighting their distinct features, traditional practices, and contributions to the country's vibrant cultural mosaic.

Swahili Culture:

The Swahili people, primarily found along the coastal regions of Kenya, have a distinct culture influenced by centuries of trade and interaction with Arab, Persian, and Indian merchants. Swahili culture is a fusion of Bantu traditions and Islamic influences, evident in their language, cuisine, architecture, and music. Swahili architecture, with its ornate door carvings and distinctive coral stone houses, is a testament to their cultural identity. The vibrant coastal cuisine, such as pilau (spiced rice) and biryani, reflects the fusion of African and Arabic flavours.

Maasai Culture:

The Maasai people, known for their semi-nomadic lifestyle, inhabit the southern regions of Kenya. They are renowned for their distinct attire, characterised by brightly coloured shukas (cloths), intricate beadwork, and elaborate jewellery. The Maasai are proud cattle herders, and their communities revolve around livestock. Their traditional ceremonies, such as the elaborate rite of passage for young warriors (Morans), showcase their cultural values, music, dance, and storytelling.

Masai Culture dancing and jumping Source: www.nathab.com

Kikuyu Culture

The Kikuyu, the largest ethnic group in Kenya, reside mainly in the Central Highlands. The Kikuyu (also Agĩkũyũ/Gĩkũyũ) are a Bantu ethnic group native to Central Kenya. At a population of 8,148,668 as of 2019, they account for 17.13% of the total population of Kenya, making them Kenya's largest ethnic group. The term Kikuyu is derived from the Swahili form of the word Gĩkũyũ. Gĩkũyũ is derived from the word mũkũyũ which means "sycamore fig (mũkũyũ) tree". Hence Agĩkũyũ in the Kikuyu language translates to "Children Of The Big Sycamore".

Agriculture forms the backbone of their economy, and their cultural practices are deeply intertwined with farming traditions. The Kikuyu people have a rich oral tradition, with stories, proverbs, and folklore passed down through generations. The traditional circumcision ceremony for boys (Iria) and elaborate weddings are significant cultural events that highlight the community's customs and values.

Kikuyu Culture Source www.tuko.co.ke

Luo Culture:

The Luo people, living around Lake Victoria and in western Kenya, have a vibrant culture known for its music, dance, and storytelling. The Luo of Kenya and Tanzania are a Nilotic ethnic group native to western Kenya and the Mara Region of northern Tanzania in East Africa. The Luo are the fourth-largest ethnic group (10.65%) in Kenya. The Luo descended from migrants who moved into western Kenya from Uganda between the 15th and 20th centuries in four waves. These migrants were closely related to Luo peoples found in Uganda, especially the Acholi and Padhola peoples. As they moved into Kenya and Tanzania, they underwent significant genetic and cultural admixture as they encountered other communities that were long established in the region.

Traditionally, Luo people practised a mixed economy of cattle pastoralism, seed farming and fishing supplemented by hunting. Today, the Luo comprise a significant fraction of East Africa's intellectual and skilled labour force in various professions. They also engage in various trades, such as tenant fishing, small-scale farming, and urban work. The Luo also have unique traditional costumes and rituals associated with birth, marriage, and death.

Luhya Culture:

The Luhya (also known as Abaluyia or Luyia) are a Bantu ethnic group in Kenya. They number about 5.3 million people, being about 16% of Kenya's total population of 38.5 million, and are the second-largest ethnic group in Kenya. Luhya refers to both the people and their language.

Luhya culture Source: http://www.johntyman.com/

The Luhya community, comprising over 16 subgroups, occupies the western regions of Kenya. They are known for their agricultural practices, with each subgroup specialising in different crops.

Luhya culture emphasises communal values, and traditional ceremonies, such as the circumcision rites (Bukusu) and bullfighting (Isikuti), are significant cultural events. The Luhya people also excel in traditional music, dance, and storytelling.

Turkana Culture:

The Turkana are a Nilotic people native to the Turkana County in northwest Kenya, a semi-arid climate region bordering Lake Turkana in the east; Pokot, Rendille and Samburu people to the south; Uganda to the west; and South Sudan (Didinga and Toposa) and Ethiopia to the north.

According to the 2019 Kenyan census, Turkana number 1,016,174, or 2.14% of the Kenyan population, making it the tenth largest ethnicity in Kenya. They refer to themselves as ŋiTurkana (i. e. ngiTurkana, meaning the Turkana, or people of Turkan) and to their land as "Turkan". The language of the Turkana, an Eastern Nilotic language, is also called Turkana; their own name for it is ŋaTurkana or aŋajep a ŋiTurkana.

They are mainly semi-nomadic pastoralists and are noted for raising camels and weaving baskets. In their oral traditions, they designate themselves as the people of the grey bull, the Zebu, whose domestication played an important role in their history. The Turkana people, residing in the arid regions of northern Kenya, have a unique cultural heritage shaped by their harsh environment.

2.3 ETHNIC GROUPS AND LANGUAGES

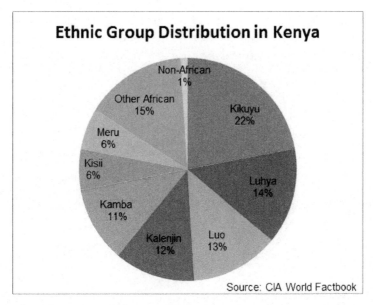

Kenya: Ethnic Group Distribution Source: CIA World Factbook

2.4 RELIGION

The Kenyan constitution guarantees freedom of religion. Around half the population are Christians, 10% are Muslim, and there are small Hindu and Sikh minorities.

Christians, including Protestants, Catholics, and others, account for 83% of Kenya's population. Muslims and followers of traditional African religions also have a significant presence in the country. Many Kenyans incorporate their indigenous religious beliefs into their practices of Christianity or Islam. Belief in ancestral spirits is strong in the country. Diviners are believed to be the link between the spirit world and the real world and are highly regarded in Kenyan society. They are often called to ward off evil spirits or cure diseases. Belief in witchcraft and reincarnation is strong in society. The balance of the population follows traditional African, often animist, beliefs. Christians tend to be concentrated in the west and central sections of the country, while Muslims cluster in the eastern coastal regions.

Kenya religious affiliation (2019)

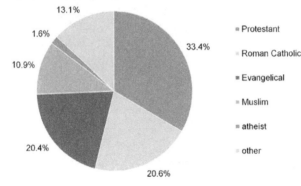

© Encyclopædia Britannica, Inc.

Kenya Religious affiliation (2019) Source: Encyclopedia Britannica

2.5 SETTLEMENT PATTERNS

Most of Kenya's population is rural and lives in scattered settlements, the location and concentration of which depend largely on climatic and soil conditions. Before European colonisation, virtually no villages or towns existed except along the coast. At the same time, urbanisation was confined to fishing villages, Arab trading ports, and towns visited by dhows from the Arabian Peninsula and Asia. The migration from rural to urban areas has accelerated since independence, spurred by greater economic development in urban areas. In the late 1960s, about one-tenth of the national population lived in urban areas of 1,000 or more people; by the turn of the 21st century, the figure had more than doubled. The largest coastal city is Mombasa, while most Kenyans in the interior live in the capital city, Nairobi. The influx of people has placed a significant burden on providing such services as education, health and sanitation, water, and electricity.

2.6 DEMOGRAPHIC TRENDS

Kenya age breakdown (2019)

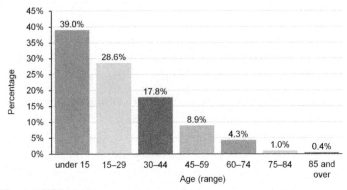

© Encyclopædia Britannica, Inc.

Kenya Age breakdown Source: Encyclopedia Britannica

Kenya's accelerating population growth from the early 1960s to the early 1980s seriously constrained the country's social and economic development. During the first quarter of the 20th century, the population was fewer than four million, largely because of famines, wars, and disease. By the late 1940s, the population had risen to more than five million; at independence in 1963, it was more than eight million and growing rapidly. The population exceeded 20 million by the mid-1980s, and the growth rate slowed dramatically.

Nonetheless, in the early 21st century, the rate of natural increase was still above the world average. As some two-thirds of Kenyans were under age 30, the country's higher-than-average growth rate was expected to continue for some time. The pressure of such a population explosion produced limited employment opportunities; rising costs for education, health services, and food imports; and an inability to generate the resources to build housing in both urban and rural areas. The most important causes of the country's explosive population growth were a sharp fall in mortality rates—especially infant mortality—and the traditional preference for large families.

Group Orientation

Kenyans are group-orientated rather than individualistic. "Harambee," (coming from the Bantu word meaning "to pull together") defines the people's approach to others in life.

The concept is about mutual assistance, mutual effort, mutual responsibility, and community self-reliance. This principle has historically been practised by every ethnic group, with its roots in cooperative farming or herding. Harambee took on a more political resonance when used at the time of independence by Jomo Kenyatta as a way to bring people together.

As you might expect in a group-orientated culture, the extended family is the basis of the social structure. Family in Kenya is not just the nuclear family but extends to cousins, uncles, and aunts. In Kenyan culture, family is considered a major factor in identity, a sense of belonging, and security. The upbringing of a child in Kenya means cousins, aunts, and uncles play a large role in their day-to-day life who may make visits without prior notice and expect a helping hand when in need.

The husband's parents often live with the nuclear family when they age and can no longer care for themselves. When people marry, they join their families, thus ensuring that there will always be a group to turn to in times of need.

Dinner is an important meal as it brings together all family members. Religious services are also a communal experience for families, and religious beliefs are strong for Christian, Muslim and

Hindu communities. Sunday is the biggest day for Christian families as they spend almost all day in church activities.

In Kenya, household chores are traditionally done by women. Sometimes men try to help in the house, but it's uncommon. Children are generally expected to make their beds each morning and tidy up their rooms.

Kenyan culture is very communal. Kenyans share everything from clothes food, and even space! At home, personal items are often shared with every family member. Most families don't understand the concept of private time, and it's uncommon to stay alone in one's room for long periods of time except to sleep.

Ancestors

Like most Africans, Kenyans greatly emphasise the respect and reverence of their deceased ancestors. This is not ancestor worship per se, but rather a belief that when someone dies, their spirit lives on and must be acknowledged. The belief is that the person only dies completely when their relatives no longer remember them.

One's ancestors are thought to be able to influence events in life since they are in a limbo state and closer to God than the living. Therefore, people make offerings to them or name a baby after one so his spirit can live in the child. Demonstrating respect towards ancestors is believed to maintain harmonious relationships within the family, extended family, and clan or tribe.

Greetings and Respect: - Greetings are highly valued in Kenyan culture. When meeting someone, it is customary to shake hands, and it is considered polite to maintain eye contact during the greeting. A slight bow may accompany the handshake in some communities, such as the Maasai. Use appropriate titles when addressing individuals, such as "Mzee" for an elder or "Bwana" for a man, followed by his last name.

When greeting someone with whom you have a personal relationship, the handshake is more prolonged than the one given to a casual acquaintance. The most common greeting is "Jambo?" ("How are you?"), which is generally said immediately before the handshake. After the handshake, it is the norm to ask questions about the person's health, family, business and anything else you know about him. To skip or rush this element in the greeting process is the height of poor manners. Once a personal relationship has developed, you may be able to address a person by his title and first name, first name alone, or nickname. Wait for the Kenyan to determine that your friendship has reached this level of intimacy.

People are generally addressed by their academic, professional, or honorific title followed by their surname. When greeting an elder or someone of higher status, grasp the right wrist with the left hand while shaking hands to demonstrate respect.

Close female friends may hug and kiss once on each cheek instead of shaking hands. Muslim men/women do not always shake hands with men. Women over 21 are often addressed as "Mama" and men over 35 are often addressed as "Mzee". Children generally refer to adults as Aunt or Uncle, even without familial relationships.

Politeness and Humility: - Politeness and humility are highly regarded in Kenyan culture. It is customary to use "please" (tafadhali) and "thank you" (asante) when making requests or expressing gratitude. Modesty is appreciated, so boasting or bragging about personal achievements is considered impolite.

Gift Giving: - Gift giving is a common practice in Kenyan culture, particularly during special occasions or as a token of appreciation. When presenting a gift, it is polite to do so with both hands. Gifts are typically opened privately, not in the giver's presence, to avoid potential embarrassment.

Kenyans generally give gifts for events of significance in a person's life or days of religious significance. Gifts need not be expensive, and practical gifts are preferred. Kenya is a poor country, and a gift of something that the person cannot generally afford is always welcome.

Giving small gifts to servants, tradespeople, and service workers at Christmas is customary.

Bring pastries, flowers, or sweets for the hostess if invited to dinner at a Kenyan's home. In rural areas, gifts of sugar or tea are quite common.

Gifts should be nicely wrapped, although there are no prohibitions concerning paper colour. Do not bring alcohol unless you know that your host drinks. Gifts should be given using the right hand only or both hands. Never use the left hand.

Dining Etiquette: - If invited to someone's home for a meal, removing your shoes before entering is customary unless otherwise indicated. Wash your hands before eating, as many traditional meals are eaten with the hands. Utensils may be provided for those who prefer to use them. It is polite to try a little of everything served and to finish what is on your plate as a sign of appreciation—tipping the waitstaff if dining out is customary, although the amount may vary.

Kenyans' table manners are relatively formal, and dining patterns vary tremendously according to the host's ethnicity, location, and socio-economic position. The best course of action is to behave formally. When in doubt, watch what others are doing and follow their lead.

Except for formal functions, there is generally no seating plan. However, there may be a special place for the most honoured guest. Guests are expected to wash their hands before and after the meal. In some homes, a washing basin will be brought to the table. If so, hold your hands over the basin while water is poured over them.

The honoured guest is usually served first, followed by the men, children, and women.

Servants often bring the courses to individual guests who are expected to take what they want.

Do not begin eating until the eldest male has been served and started eating. It is a good idea to take a small amount the first time the platters are brought so that you may take second helpings when urged.

Beverages are not generally served with meals since Kenyans think it is impolite to eat and drink simultaneously. They are generally served after the meal, and finishing everything on your plate is considered polite, although it is not mandatory.

Dress Code: - Kenyan dress code varies depending on the region and occasion. In urban areas, Western-style clothing is commonly worn. However, modest attire is expected in rural and more traditional communities, especially when visiting religious sites or attending cultural ceremonies. It is advisable to dress respectfully, avoiding revealing or provocative clothing.

Language and Communication: English and Swahili are the official languages of Kenya, with various ethnic languages spoken across the country. When interacting with locals, using simple greetings or phrases in Swahili, such as "Jambo" (hello) or "Asante sana" (thank you very much), is appreciated and shows respect for the local culture.

Respect for Elders and Authority: - Respect for elders and those in positions of authority is deeply ingrained in Kenyan culture. It is important to show deference and use appropriate language and gestures when addressing older individuals or authority figures.

Elders are often consulted for advice and their opinions are highly valued in decision-making.

Cultural Sensitivity: - Kenya's cultural diversity should be embraced and respected. Being sensitive to different customs, practices, and beliefs is important. Seek permission before taking photographs, especially in rural areas or during cultural events. Avoid discussions on sensitive topics, such as politics or tribal conflicts, unless the locals initiate the conversation.

By understanding and respecting Kenyan etiquette and customs, visitors and foreigners can forge positive connections, build relationships, and immerse themselves in the vibrant cultural tapestry of the country. Embracing these customs showcases an appreciation for the local traditions and contributes to a memorable and meaningful experience in Kenya.

2.7 FAMILY LIFE IN KENYA

Kenyan society is a patriarchal society where men primarily control money and property. Women, however, usually work more than men. In rural areas, women manage the household and children, work in the fields, maintain a vegetable garden, cook, and sell food in the market. Village men often leave their homes to migrate to the cities for paid work. In urban areas, women constitute nearly 40% of the workforce. Despite their significant contributions, women still earn relatively less than men and hold lower-paying jobs. Domestic violence is common in Kenya, wife beating is prevalent, and women have little legal help to deal with such issues. Another major problem plaguing Kenyan women is female genital mutilation, making them susceptible to pain and infections. Today, however, many women's rights organisations are working hard to get the rights of women recognised.

Marriages in Kenya are usually arranged. The tradition of polygamy is still practised today but is becoming rarer. In polygamous households, the multiple wives are usually assigned separate huts where they live with their children while the man has a hut for himself. In urban areas, monogamous marriages are more common and nuclear families are growing in number. Men pay a bride's price to the bride's family in exchange for their daughter. The bride price is generally higher for the first wife than for subsequent ones. Inheritance is patrilineal.

Children are highly valued in Kenyan families, and the entire community, including immediate and extended family members, is responsible for rearing children. Boys and girls have different upbringings and are taught gender-appropriate roles at an early age. Primary education is free in Kenya. However, literacy rates are low in the country, and its education system is considered poor quality.

Kenyans are considered to be very hospitable and friendly people who value social interactions a lot. Greetings are extended in nature when one shakes hands or hugs and asks about health and family members. Visitors to Kenyan homes are almost always well-fed by the host family. Older people are treated with a lot of respect.

2.8 FEMALE GENITAL MUTILATION (FGM) IN KENYA

Female genital mutilation (FGM), also known as female genital cutting, is a deeply rooted cultural practice prevalent in some communities in Kenya. It involves the partial or total removal of the external female genitalia for non-medical reasons. While FGM is not specific to Kenya and is practised in several countries, including other African nations, it is important to shed light on its cultural context within Kenya.

FGM in Kenya is primarily practised among certain ethnic groups, including the Maasai, Samburu, Kuria, Pokot, and Somali communities. The practice is often steeped in cultural and traditional beliefs, including notions of purity, femininity, marriageability, and adherence to social norms. Some of the commonly cited reasons for practising FGM in these communities include preserving virginity, ensuring marital fidelity, enhancing cleanliness, and upholding cultural identity.

However, it is crucial to note that FGM is internationally recognised as a human rights violation and poses severe health risks to women and girls. The procedure can lead to immediate complications, such as severe pain, bleeding, infection, and even death. It can also result in long-term physical, psychological, and sexual consequences, including chronic pain, complications during childbirth, and trauma.

Efforts to address FGM in Kenya have been ongoing for decades, both from the government and civil society organisations. The Prohibition of Female Genital Mutilation Act was enacted in 2011, making the practice illegal in Kenya. Additionally, various campaigns, advocacy initiatives, community dialogues, and education programs have been implemented to raise awareness about the harmful effects of FGM and promote its abandonment.

Despite these efforts, eliminating FGM remains a complex challenge deeply intertwined with cultural, social, and economic factors. The practice persists due to deeply ingrained beliefs, community pressure, and the lack of alternative rites of passage for girls. Overcoming FGM requires a comprehensive approach involving community engagement, education, empowerment of women and girls, and addressing the underlying socio-cultural norms and beliefs perpetuating the practice.

It is important to note that not all communities in Kenya practice FGM, and many individuals within practising communities are actively working towards its eradication. The Kenyan government and civil society organisations continue to collaborate to protect the rights and well-being of girls and women and to foster cultural change that promotes gender equality and the abandonment of harmful practices like FGM.

2.9 POLYGAMY IN KENYA

Polygamy, the practice of having multiple spouses simultaneously, has a long history and cultural significance in many parts of the world, including Kenya. In Kenya, polygamy has deep roots in traditional African customs predating the colonial era and is a prevalent form of marital union.

Traditional African societies often practised polygamy to establish alliances, ensure societal stability, and support agricultural economies. Polygamy was regarded as a symbol of wealth, power, and status, with men able to marry multiple wives to expand their households and enhance their social standing.

Polygamy is often viewed as preserving ancestral traditions and ensuring lineage continuity. Polygamous marriages are seen as a means to strengthen family ties, foster cooperation, and provide emotional and financial support within extended families. Moreover, the practice of polygamy is sometimes associated with religious beliefs and is recognized as permissible under Islamic law.

From a legal perspective, Kenya recognizes polygamous marriages under certain circumstances. The country's Marriage Act of 2014 provides guidelines for both monogamous and polygamous unions. According to the law, a man can enter into a polygamous marriage if he can prove that he has the means to support multiple wives and that the subsequent wives consent to the arrangement. However, polygamy is not recognized in civil law and carries no legal consequences in terms of inheritance and property rights.

As Kenya undergoes rapid social and cultural changes, the perception and practice of polygamy have evolved. While some individuals still embrace polygamy as a choice that aligns with their cultural values and traditions, others challenge its relevance in modern society. Critics argue polygamy can perpetuate gender inequalities, as women may face unequal treatment, limited autonomy, and emotional distress within such unions. The economic pressures and financial burden of supporting multiple households can also strain family resources.

Furthermore, increased urbanization, westernization, and education have influenced a shift in attitudes toward polygamy. Many younger Kenyans, particularly those in urban areas, choose monogamous marriages as they prioritize personal aspirations, gender equality, and companionship over traditional practices.

To navigate the challenges and opportunities polygamy presents in Kenya, promoting dialogue and awareness around the practice is essential. Education is crucial in empowering individuals, particularly women, to make informed choices about their relationships and challenge harmful gender norms.

Efforts should be made to provide comprehensive sexuality education that includes discussions on healthy relationships, consent, gender equality, and the rights of individuals within marriages. By promoting gender equality and emphasizing the importance of mutual respect and consent, society can work towards reducing the negative consequences associated with polygamy.

It is also important to address the economic implications of polygamous marriages. Providing support and resources to individuals in polygamous unions can help alleviate financial strain and improve the overall well-being of all family members. This could include initiatives such as vocational training, access to microfinance, and business development programs, which can empower individuals to generate income and support their families.

Additionally, legal reforms and safeguards are necessary to protect the rights of individuals in polygamous marriages. Ensuring that women have equal rights to property, inheritance, and decision-making within the family unit is crucial. Establishing mechanisms for resolving conflicts and addressing domestic violence within polygamous marriages is also essential.

Moreover, engaging religious and community leaders in conversations about polygamy can help foster a more inclusive and progressive understanding of marital relationships. By promoting alternative interpretations of religious texts and encouraging dialogue on gender equality, religious leaders can play a vital role in challenging harmful practices and promoting healthy relationships.

In conclusion, polygamy in Kenya is a complex issue deeply rooted in history, culture, and tradition. While it continues to be a significant part of many Kenyan communities, evolving social dynamics and changing attitudes necessitate a thoughtful and balanced approach. By promoting education, gender equality, legal reforms, and engaging religious and community leaders, Kenya can strive for a society where individuals have the freedom to choose their marital arrangements while ensuring the well-being and rights of all involved.

2.10 SOCIAL LIFE IN KENYA

Kenyans flood the coast during major holidays: - Every time there is a major season/ holiday in Kenya, including the Christmas, New Year, and Easter holidays, the Kenyan coast will be bursting as it seems with all the people visiting from Nairobi and other major cities in the country.

Mombasa, Malindi, and Lamu are some of the preferred holiday destinations for many Kenyans looking to have some fun on the sandy beaches and in the beautiful hotels.

Seafront hotels and restaurants enjoy booming businesses during this time as their hotels are always booked to capacity, so if you are planning a trip to Kenya around this time, you might want to make reservations way before you get here.

Alcohol is a way of life: - Kenyans love their alcohol just like they love their tea. After a long day at work, many Kenyans flock to their local bars or nightclubs in Nairobi for a cold beer while catching up with friends or watching a game. Kenyans also love to make an alcoholic drink they call "Dawa". This is a cocktail whose main ingredient is vodka. Alcohol brings Kenyans together, especially when there are major football games (especially European premier league games) on the television.

Security checks are the order of the day: - Security checks in Kenya have become a tradition, especially with the regular terrorism threats. Unfortunately, several people have lost their lives to terrorists recently, so security is a big issue everywhere you go in Kenya.

You cannot enter a building, especially those in major cities, without being frisked. This is especially true in Kenyan malls where trained police search you; dogs are trained to detect anything suspicious, whether on you or in your vehicle.

In addition, when you come to Kenya for the first time, you will notice that almost all houses and apartments have their own enclosures. These are mostly protective stone walls with barbed wires at the top or broken pieces of glass arranged so that they can cut you if you try to jump over the fence.

Polygamy is legal in Kenya: - Kenya's parliament passed a bill allowing its men to marry multiple wives in March 2014. This bill, officially signed into law, finally recognised what had long been a cultural practice in the country. Many male Members of Parliament supported the bill, allowing Kenyan men to take more wives without consulting existing spouses.

"Kaa chonjo" is a phrase you must understand: - "Kaa chonjo" means always alert. You always have to be alert when in Kenya for many reasons. From using public vehicles to the water and electricity and even cooking gas in your house, to the people you hire to work for you in your home, to the places you choose to live in. You should always be aware of your surroundings.

For example, if you are in public transport that is speeding or being driven carelessly, always "Zusha!" (Make noise).

For the Luo Community, mourning the dead is an elaborate affair: - Mourning the dead is an extravagant ceremony among the Luo people of Kenya. The Luo have explained this as a way of showing respect to the dead, a final befitting send-off. When a Luo dies, mourning starts immediately, lasting several days or weeks. The mourning is defined by singing and dancing meant to chase away the spirits of death.

The extravagance of a mourning ceremony will depend on many factors, including the gender of the deceased, the age, marital and social status, the circumstance of their death, and even the area they come from.

Enuoto, an event of shaving the Morans, is a once-in-a-lifetime ceremony for the Maasai Community. - The Maasai are one of the most popular tribes of Kenya, especially with tourists, as they are the one group that has maintained many of their traditions. However, they have many more traditions, including the shaving of the Morans (Warriors), an event that sees young Maasai warriors transition into senior community warriors. This event is referred to as "Enuoto". Enuoto is a once-in-a-lifetime ceremony.

Any Moran who does not go through this ceremony is not allowed to marry. Bulls are also slaughtered during the event, and a traditional brew ("Enasho") made from a combination of honey and aloe roots is served to the elders and the graduating Morans.

For the Kipsigis Community, the land is given to their unmarried: - Unlike many Kenyan communities whose cultures do not allow their women to be given land, the situation is different when it comes to the Kipsigis community. In this community, women can be allocated land by their parents or brothers in case they fail to get married. When a woman has reached her prime age, and with no potential suitors chasing after her, her family is allowed to give her a piece of land to settle on where she can farm and build a house for herself. If she gets children, they are the ones that inherit that piece of land if she passes on.

For the Bukusu Community, traditional circumcision is still the norm: - Circumcision (cutting off of the foreskin) is a rite of passage for many Kenyan men. How it is done varies with whether you live in the city or the village, and it also varies greatly from one community to the other.

Circumcision, however, becomes more interesting when you compare how different communities do it.

For the Bukusu, a sub-tribe of the Luhya community, the young initiates (usually boys between the ages of 12 to 14) are woken up at 3 am and escorted to a river. They are then made to strip and stay in the water until their bodies become numb. Mud is then applied all over their bodies. The entire village gathers around them (no women are allowed close to the river) as they stand with their feet firmly on the ground, their eyes facing the sky, and their arms resting on their sides as they are being circumcised.

During the circumcision, you are not allowed to flinch, wince or cringe because by doing so, you will be committing the ultimate form of cowardice and become the village's laughing stock. Additionally, no girl will want to marry you to avoid the reputation of having married a coward.

For the Luo Community, wife inheritance is still a thing: - A Luo proverb says "Dhako chogo morudore gik libamba jok modong'to gweno". This translates to "A woman is a middle bone that the clan chews after her husband's death" and is the proverb from which the inheritance of a wife is derived .

CHAPTER 3
KENYAN BUSINESS ETIQUETTE

UNDERSTANDING KENYA'S business culture and etiquette is crucial for establishing successful relationships and conducting business effectively. As a diverse country, Kenya exhibits a blend of traditional and modern business practices. Here are key aspects to consider when engaging in business in Kenya:

Culture and society are integral components of Kenya's identity and heritage. The country is home to over 40 different ethnic groups, each with its own unique traditions, languages, and customs.

Kenya's cultural landscape is shaped by a rich history of migration and trade and centuries of colonial rule. The country's ethnic groups are spread throughout, with the most prominent groups including the Kikuyu, Luo, Kalenjin, and Luhya. Each of these groups has its own distinct language and customs, and many also have their own traditional dress, music, and dance.

Kenyan society is deeply influenced by its cultural traditions, particularly in rural areas where many people live according to traditional customs and practices. These customs often centre around family and community, strongly emphasising hospitality, respect for elders, and communal living. Traditional practices such as dowry payments, circumcision, and initiation ceremonies are important in many Kenyan communities.

As is true for many developing African countries, there is a marked contrast between urban and rural culture in Kenya. Kenya's cities are characterised by a more cosmopolitan population whose tastes reflect practices that combine the local with the global. Nairobi's nightlife, for instance, caters to youth interested in music that varies from American rhythm and blues, hip-hop, and rock to Congolese rumba. The city contains movie theatres and numerous nightclubs where patrons can dance or shoot pool; there are water parks and family amusement centres for children.

At the same time, Kenya's society is also shaped by contemporary social issues such as urbanisation, globalisation, and the ongoing struggle for gender equality. Urbanisation, in particular, has profoundly impacted Kenyan society, with many young people leaving rural areas for better economic opportunities. This has led to the growth of urban slums and informal settlements, which often lack basic services such as clean water, sanitation, and healthcare.

However, traditional practices remain important for the modernisation and urbanisation of Kenya. Rituals and customs are very well documented, thanks to the intense anthropological study of Kenya's peoples during British colonial rule; oral literature is safeguarded, and several publishing houses publish traditional folktales and ethnographies.

One of Kenya's most prominent social customs is the important role of family and community. Families are considered the building blocks of society, and there is a strong emphasis on extended family relationships, with many people living close to their relatives. This has contributed to a strong sense of community and social cohesion in many parts of the country.

Kenyans are known for their warmth and welcoming nature and it is common for visitors to be offered food and drink as a sign of respect and hospitality. This custom is deeply ingrained in Kenyan culture and is seen as a way of building and maintaining social relationships.

In addition to social customs, daily life in Kenya is shaped by various factors, including economic conditions, political developments, and environmental challenges. Poverty and inequality remain significant challenges for many Kenyans, particularly those living in rural areas or informal settlements in urban centres. Climate change and environmental degradation have also impacted the country, leading to various challenges, including droughts, floods, and soil erosion.

Urban life in Kenya is by no means uniform. For example, as a Muslim town, Mombasa stands in contrast to Nairobi. Although there are numerous restaurants, bars, and clubs in Mombasa, there are also many mosques and women dressed in bui buis (loose-fitting garments that cover married Muslim women from head to toe) are common.

Rural life is oriented in two directions—toward the lifestyles of rural inhabitants, who still constitute the majority of Kenya's population, and toward foreign tourists who visit the many national parks and reserves. Although agricultural duties occupy most of the time of rural dwellers, they still find occasions to visit markets and shopping centres, where some frequent beer halls. Mobile cinemas also provide entertainment for the rural population.

Kenya observes most Christian holidays and the Muslim festival Eid al-Fitr, which marks the end of Ramadan. Jamhuri, or Independence Day, is celebrated on December 12. Moi Day (recognising Daniel arap Moi) and Kenyatta Day, both in October, honour two of the country's presidents, while Madaraka (Swahili:

Government) Day on June 1 celebrates Kenya's attainment of self-governance in 1964.

One of the most vibrant aspects of Kenyan culture is its music and dance. Music plays an important role in traditional ceremonies, such as weddings, funerals, and initiation rites, and many Kenyan communities have their own unique styles of music and dance. For example, the Luo people are known for their "Benga" music, while the Kikuyu people have their own style of folk music called "Mugithi."

In addition to traditional music, Kenya has also produced many internationally renowned musicians, including Sauti Sol, Eric Wainaina, and Ayub Ogada. These musicians have incorporated elements of traditional Kenyan music into their own styles, creating a fusion of traditional and contemporary sounds that is uniquely Kenyan.

Kenya's art scene is also thriving, with a growing number of galleries, museums, and cultural institutions showcasing the work of Kenyan artists. Kenya's art scene is diverse and vibrant, from traditional crafts like beadwork and basket weaving to contemporary art forms such as painting, sculpture, and photography.

Kenya's society is also marked by its diversity of languages. While Swahili and English are the two official languages, over 60 indigenous languages are spoken nationwide. This linguistic diversity reflects Kenya's complex history of migration and trade and has led to ongoing efforts to preserve and promote these languages.

Kenya is also home to several unique cultural practices, such as "nyama choma," a traditional barbecue-style meal popular throughout the country. Another popular cultural event is the "Maasai Mara," an annual migration of wildebeest and other animals between Kenya and Tanzania.

Communication Style

Direct and frank communication is not the norm in Kenya. Kenyans will always attempt to qualify what they say so that the message is delivered sensitively in order to protect people's faces and the relationship. If the relationship is intimate, the communication style will become more direct. Diplomacy will be of utmost importance for newly established and more formal relationships.

In their attempt not to cause problems, Kenyans often use metaphors, analogies, and stories to make a point. They are uncomfortable with blunt statements. You may wish to moderate your delivery style if you are from a culture that prizes directness. It is also up to you to read between the lines and decipher what may really be said. With this in mind, criticism should be delivered in private and given in a circumspect manner.

Kenyans may gesture for emphasis when speaking. Loud voices are generally only used during disagreements in business situations, although louder speaking tones are the norm in rural areas. Showing anger is considered a sign of mental instability. Kenyans pride themselves on their emotional control and expect the same from others.

Since maintaining honour and dignity are paramount, Kenyans may offer what they believe is the expected response rather than to say something that might embarrass the other person.

They often go out of their way to keep from doing something that could bring shame to another person. They expect business colleagues and superiors to inquire about their families before beginning a business discussion.

Meeting and Greeting

Handshakes are the most common greeting in business. When being introduced to someone for the first time, the handshake is short, while handshakes among people with a personal relationship are longer.

It is a sign of respect to lower your eyes when greeting someone of higher status or someone who is older than you. Men should wait for a woman to extend her hand first.

To rush a greeting is extremely rude. Take the time to inquire about the other person's general well-being, family, and business in general. Titles are important; use the honorific title, any academic or professional title, and surname.

Wait to be invited before moving to a first-name basis. Business cards are exchanged without formal ritual. Present and receive business cards with two hands.

3.1 KENYAN BUSINESS CULTURE

The structure and formality of meetings vary depending on the company's ownership. British or Indian-owned companies generally follow agendas for their meetings. Regarding formal meetings, confirming the meeting time and date a few days in advance is crucial. This practice holds significance in ensuring proper coordination.

In Kenya, where building relationships is valued, you should allocate time for small talk to acquaint yourself with your hosts and vice versa. Let your Kenyan host decide when he considers it to be the appropriate time to transition to the business discussion. Within Kenyan business culture, titles carry weight. Individuals address each other using academic, professional, or honorific titles, followed by surnames. It is advisable to wait for your Kenyan counterpart to determine when a higher level of informality is acceptable .

Meetings in Kenya generally do not have strict ending times. The focus is on reaching a satisfactory conclusion for all involved parties. Kenyans find the concept of an explicit ending time amusing, as they believe the meeting concludes only when everyone is satisfied. Typically, meetings commence and conclude with handshakes, exchange of business cards, and engaging in small talk.

To formally commence a meeting, each participant will stand and introduce themselves to everyone present. Seating arrangements in meetings usually reflect the hierarchy of the attendees. Business meetings in Kenya tend to be lengthy as everyone is expected to contribute to the discussions.

In the public sector, decisions are typically made by superiors and then passed down to employees. Conversely, employees are encouraged to generate ideas in the private sector, but superiors make the final decisions. Large meetings often include a coffee break, while smaller meetings may offer coffee or tea during the session.

Most meetings and negotiations in Kenya are conducted in English.

Respect

Respect is integral to successful business dealings in Kenya. For example, to greet someone of higher status in a business setting is a sign of deference and respect to lower one's eyes and supports the right forearm with the left hand while shaking hands.

This greeting is usually accompanied by asking general questions about the well-being of the person, his family, and the business. Skipping or rushing this form of greeting is perceived as poor etiquette. During meetings, everyone is provided with an opportunity to contribute to the meeting. Every remark, criticism or suggestion is given consideration. Thus, to build rapport with your Kenyan business counterpart, respect everyone present at the meeting by listening to their thoughts and by showing deference to those of higher standing.

Considerations

Business operations in Kenya are often influenced by what is known as 'Swahili Time'. This means that if a meeting is scheduled to begin at, let's say, 7:00 am, it is common for it actually to start closer to 8:00 am. Consequently, arriving late for a business meeting is generally tolerated, especially if you inform the participants beforehand about the possibility of your delay.

However, employees tend to make a concerted effort to arrive on time for work. Many factors in potential delays with public transportation and allocate more than sufficient time for their commute. English is widely spoken, particularly in the business context, and is a common language for communication. In Kenyan business culture, a high level of importance is placed on education. Regardless of an individual's work experience, those with a higher level of education are held in high esteem by others.

Business practices can differ across different regions. For instance, business activities in the capital city of Nairobi are often fast-paced. In contrast, in the coastal city of Mombasa, business transactions tend to proceed at a more leisurely pace.

Many Kenyan businesses prioritise 'Corporate Social Responsibility (CSR). This can take various forms, such as contributing to the local community, initiating social and environmental projects, or promoting Kenyan culture. Any assistance provided to a Kenyan company pursuing CSR would be greatly appreciated. Most of Kenya's labour force work outside the formal sector, either as subsistence farmers or in the urban informal sector. On the Corruption Perception Index (2017), Kenya ranks 143rd out of 180 countries, receiving a score of 28 (on a scale from 0 to 100). This perception suggests that the country's public sector is somewhat corrupt.

Relationship Building: Building strong relationships is highly valued in Kenyan business culture. Take the time to establish personal connections and engage in small talk before diving into business matters. Developing trust and rapport is essential for successful partnerships and negotiations.

Business Attire: Dress conservatively and professionally in business settings. Men typically wear suits or smart attire, while women opt for modest and formal clothing. It is essential to consider cultural norms and to dress respectfully, especially when conducting business outside major cities.

Business Cards and Exchanges: Exchanging business cards is a common practice in Kenya. Ensure that your business cards include your job title and qualifications. When receiving a business card, show respect by accepting it with both hands and reviewing it before putting it away.

Business Meetings and Negotiations: Prepare an agenda in advance and share it with your Kenyan counterparts. Meetings may begin with some small talk, and it is important to be patient and allow for informal discussions. Kenyan business culture emphasises consensus-building and group decision-making. Avoid rushing the negotiations and be prepared for multiple meetings to build trust and reach agreements.

Gift Giving and Hospitality: Gift giving is not essential in Kenyan business culture but can be appreciated as a goodwill gesture. If presenting a gift, opt for something of value or significance. When invited to someone's home, it is customary to bring a small gift, such as flowers or chocolates, to show appreciation for the hospitality.

Business Socialising: Kenyan business culture often involves socialising outside formal business settings. Accept invitations to meals or cultural events, as these provide opportunities to build relationships further. Respect local customs and traditions during such occasions.

Follow-up and Professionalism: After business meetings or negotiations, it is important to follow up promptly with any agreed-upon actions or documentation. Maintain professionalism in all correspondence and honour commitments made during discussions.

You can confidently navigate the local business landscape and establish fruitful relationships by embracing and respecting Kenya's business culture and etiquette. Building strong connections, demonstrating respect, and adapting to the Kenyan business environment will contribute to successful business endeavours in the country.

Ugali, served here with beef and sauce. Source www.capetocasa.com

3.2 CUISINE

There is no singular dish that represents all of Kenya's wide cuisine. Different communities have their own native foods.

Staples are maise and other cereals, depending on the region, including millet and sorghum, eaten with various meats and vegetables. The foods universally eaten in Kenya are ugali, sukuma wiki, and nyama choma. Kenya's coastal cuisine is unique and highly regarded throughout the country.

Ugali, served here with beef and sauce, is a mainstay of the cuisine throughout the African Great Lakes region.

Sukuma wiki, a Swahili phrase which means "to push the week", is a simple dish made with greens similar to kale or collards that are made with cassava leaves, sweet potato leaves, or pumpkin leaves. Its Swahili name comes from the fact that it is typically eaten to "get through the week" or "stretch the week".

Nyama choma is grilled meat, considered an unofficial national dish—usually goat or sheep—while kuku choma is grilled chicken. It is usually cooked over an open fire. Mostly it is eaten with ugali, kachumbari, maharagwe (bean stew), and mchicha (shredded spinach). It is served as a traditional meal on Christmas Day.

Among the Luhya residing in the country's western region, ingokho (chicken) with ugali is a favorite meal. Other than these, they also eat tsisaka, miroo, managu, and other dishes.

In the Rift Valley, the Kalenjin have long made mursik, which they have with kimyet (ugali) and vegetable relishes such as isageek and "socheek". Also among the Kikuyu of Central Kenya, many tubers, including ngwaci (sweet potatoes), ndūma (taro root, known in Kenya as arrowroot), ikwa (yams), and mianga (cassava) are eaten, as well as legumes like beans and a Kikuyu bean known as njahi.

Among the Luo residing on the western region around Lake Victoria, kuon (ugali) and rech (fish) is a favourites, as well as gweno (chicken), aliya" (sun-dried meat), onyoso (a type of ant), ng'wen (termitoidae), dede (grasshoppers), various birds and green vegetables; alode, such as osuga, akeyo, muto, dodo, dek, apoth and bo, are all consumed with ugali.

As you move towards the city, foods eaten by working families vary according to preference and ethnicity. Rice and stew are more common with working families, as are other dishes like chapati, a staple originating from India (similar to the flatbread paranthaj), chicken stew, etc.

Kenyan cooking reflects British, Arab, and Indian influences. Foods common throughout Kenya include ugali, a mush made from corn (maize) and often served with such greens as spinach and kale. Chapati, a fried pitalike bread of Indian origin, is served with vegetables and stew; rice is also popular. Seafood and fresh-water fish are eaten in most parts of the country and provide an important source of protein. Many vegetable stews are flavoured with coconut, spices, and chillies. Although meat traditionally is not eaten every day or is eaten only in small quantities, grilled meat and all-you-can-eat buffets specializing in game, or "bush meat," are popular. Many people utilize shambas (vegetable gardens) to supplement purchased foods. In areas inhabited by the Kikuyu, irio, a stew of peas, corn, and potatoes, is common. The Maasai, known for their herds of livestock, avoid killing their cows and instead prefer to use products yielded by the animal while it is alive, including blood drained from nonlethal wounds. They generally drink milk, often mixed with cow's blood, and eat the meat of sheep or goats rather than cows.

3.3 LITERATURE AND THE ARTS

Kenya has a rich heritage of oral and written literary works. The oral literature tradition of the country continues today in several indigenous languages. However, most of the written literature is in English and Swahili. The Story of Tambuka written by Mwengo is an epic poem from the 18th century. It is written in the Swahili language and is one of the earliest written literary works. Weep

Not, Child, a novel by Thiong'o is the first English novel to be published in the country. Many internationally famed foreign authors have described Kenya in their published works, like Out of Africa and The Flame Trees of Thika.

Kenyan literature encompasses a wide range of genres, including novels, poetry, plays, and oral literature. The country has produced renowned writers who have significantly contributed to African literature. Some notable Kenyan authors include Ngũgĩ wa Thiong'o, Meja Mwangi, Grace Ogot, and Binyavanga Wainaina. Their works often explore themes such as colonialism, post-independence struggles, identity, social justice, and the changing dynamics of Kenyan society. Kenyan literature reflects the country's diverse cultures, languages, and histories and offers powerful narratives that resonate with readers both within and outside Kenya.

Weep Not, Child

"Weep Not, Child" is a novel written by Kenyan author Ngũgĩ wa Thiong'o. Set during Kenya's struggle for independence from British colonial rule, the story explores themes of identity, education, nationalism, and the effects of colonization on individuals and society.

The novel follows the life of Njoroge, a young Kikuyu boy growing up in a rural village. Njoroge comes from a poor family but is eager to receive an education and improve his circumstances. His father, Ngotho, works hard to provide for his family, and Njoroge's older brother, Kamau, is involved in the Mau Mau rebellion against the British.

Njoroge's dream of education becomes a reality when he receives a scholarship to attend a mission school, where he meets other students from different backgrounds. However, the weight of colonialism and its oppressive effects are ever-present in the school, where African students are subjected to discrimination and devaluation of their culture.

As Njoroge navigates his educational journey, he becomes increasingly aware of the injustices faced by his people and their desire for independence. He is torn between his aspirations and the sacrifices the struggle for freedom requires. The political unrest intensifies, and the Mau Mau rebellion gains momentum, bringing violence and turmoil to Njoroge's village.

The novel delves into the complex relationships and dynamics within Njoroge's family, highlighting the generational differences in their responses to the political situation. Njoroge's father, Ngotho, represents the older generation's adherence to traditional values and British influence, while his brother, Kamau, is actively involved in the fight for independence.

As the story progresses, Njoroge's personal and family life becomes entangled with the wider political struggle. Tragedy strikes and Njoroge is forced to confront the harsh realities of colonialism, loss, and their impact on his dreams and aspirations.

"Weep Not, Child" portrays the struggles, hopes, and sacrifices of individuals and communities in the face of colonial oppression. Through the experiences of Njoroge, the novel provides a poignant exploration of the effects of colonization on personal identity, education, and the quest for freedom in Kenya's history.

Visual Arts

Kenyan visual arts encompass various artistic expressions, including painting, sculpture, photography, and mixed media. Artists draw inspiration from their cultural heritage, socio-political issues, and contemporary life. Traditional art forms like woodcarving and beadwork continue to thrive alongside more contemporary styles and techniques. Kenyan visual artists like Elimo Njau, Jak Katarikawe, and Wangechi Mutu have gained international recognition for their thought-provoking and visually captivating works.

Music and Dance:

Music and dance hold a prominent place in Kenyan culture. Traditional music styles, such as Benga, Ohangla, and Mugithi, blend with modern genres like Afro-pop, hip-hop, and gospel. Kenyan musicians often infuse their lyrics with social commentary, addressing issues such as poverty, corruption, and the quest for social change. Prominent Kenyan musicians include Sauti Sol, Eric Wainaina, Ayub Ogada, and Suzanna Owiyo. Traditional dances, such as the Maasai jumping dance or the Giriama Chakacha, are performed during celebrations, ceremonies, and cultural festivals, showcasing the country's rich cultural diversity.

Cultural Festivals and Events:

Kenya is known for its vibrant cultural festivals and events celebrating its diverse ethnic groups and traditions. The Lamu Cultural Festival, Lake Turkana Festival, and Nairobi International Book Fair are just a few examples of gatherings that showcase traditional music, dance, literature, and visual arts. These events allow artists to exhibit their talent, foster cultural exchange, and promote a deeper understanding and appreciation of Kenyan arts and culture.

In conclusion, Kenya's literature and arts are a vibrant and vital part of the country's cultural fabric. Through literature, visual arts, music, dance, and theatre, Kenyan artists capture the essence of their identity, explore social issues, and celebrate the diversity of Kenyan culture. Their creative expressions serve as powerful vehicles for storytelling, cultural preservation, and social commentary and contribute to the richness of Kenya's artistic heritage.

3.4 SPORTS

Sports in an integral part of the culture of Kenya. Both indigenous traditional and modern sports are played in the country. Here's an overview of some of the prominent sports in Kenya:

Athletics: - Kenya is renowned globally for its dominance in long-distance running. Kenyan athletes have consistently excelled in middle-distance and long-distance events, winning numerous Olympic and World Championship medals. The country's success in athletics can be attributed to factors such as high-altitude training, a culture of running, and natural talent. Kenyan athletes like Kipchoge Keino, Catherine Ndereba, and David Rudisha have become icons in the sport.

Football: - Football (soccer) is the most popular sport in Kenya, with a large following and a thriving local league. The Kenyan national football team, known as the Harambee Stars, represents the country in international competitions. While the national team has had its ups and downs, football clubs like Gor Mahia and AFC Leopards have loyal fan bases and passionate rivalries. The sport brings communities together, and local leagues provide a platform for young talent to develop their skills.

Rugby: - Rugby has gained significant popularity in Kenya, with the national rugby team, known as the Shujaa, achieving success on the global stage. Kenyan rugby players are known for their speed, agility, and physicality. The annual Safari Sevens tournament attracts international teams and showcases Kenya's sports prowess. Rugby Union and Rugby Sevens have a growing fan base, and efforts are being made to develop the sport at the grassroots level.

Boxing: - Kenya has produced notable boxers who have made their mark in the sport. Boxers like Robert Wangila, Philip Waruinge, and Conjestina Achieng have represented Kenya in international competitions and won accolades. Boxing gyms and training centers are scattered nationwide, providing opportunities for aspiring boxers to hone their skills and compete at local and international levels.

Cricket: - Cricket has a dedicated following in Kenya, especially among the Asian community. The Kenyan national cricket team has participated in major cricket events, including the Cricket World Cup. Local cricket leagues and tournaments attract passionate players and enthusiasts, contributing to the growth of the sport.

Other Sports: Other sports gaining popularity in Kenya include basketball, volleyball, hockey, and motorsports. Kenyan basketball players have made their mark in international leagues, while volleyball teams like the Kenya women's national volleyball team have achieved success in continental competitions.

In conclusion, sportplays a vital role in the Kenyan society, fostering national pride, unity, and talent development. Kenyan athletes have achieved remarkable success in athletics, football, rugby, boxing, and various other sports, earning recognition and admiration worldwide. Sports provide a platform for individuals to showcase their skills, inspire others, and represent the nation with honor and excellence.

CHAPTER 4
GEOGRAPHY OF KENYA

4.1 LAND

Physical features of Kenya

Bisected horizontally by the Equator and vertically by longitude 38° E, Kenya is bordered to the north by South Sudan and Ethiopia, to the east by Somalia and the Indian Ocean, to the south by Tanzania, and to the west by Lake Victoria and Uganda.

Kenya has wide white-sand beaches on the coast. Inland plains make up three-quarters of the country, mostly bush, covered with underbrush. In the west are the highlands, where the altitude rises from three thousand to ten thousand feet. Nairobi, Kenya's largest city and capital, is located in the central highlands. Mount Kenya is the highest point at 17,058 feet (5,200 meters). Kenya shares Lake Victoria, the largest lake in Africa and the main source of the Nile River, with Tanzania and Uganda.

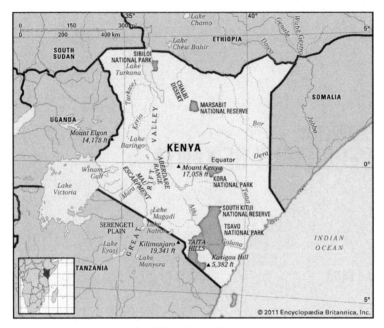

Map of Kenya Source: Britannica

Another significant feature of Kenyan geography is the Great Rift Valley, the wide, steep canyon that cuts through the highlands. Kenya is also home to some of the world's most spectacular wildlife, including elephants, lions, giraffes, zebras, antelopes, wildebeests, and many rare and beautiful species of birds. Unfortunately, the animal population is threatened by both hunting and an expanding human population; wildlife numbers fell drastically through the twentieth century. The government has introduced strict legislation regulating hunting and established a national park system to protect wildlife.

Kenya's Flag

Flag of Kenya Source: https://libertyflagandbanner.com

Symbolism. The Kenyan flag has three horizontal stripes—red, black, and green—separated by thin white bands. The black symbolizes the people of Kenya, the red represents the bloodshed in the fight for independence, and the green symbolizes agriculture. In the centre of the flag is a red shield with black and white markings and two crossed spears, which stands for vigilance to defend freedom.

Location - The 38th meridian divides Kenya into two halves of striking contrasts. While the eastern half slopes gently to the coral-backed seashore, the western portion rises abruptly through a series of hills and plateaus to the Eastern Rift Valley, known in Kenya as the Central Rift. West of the Rift is a westward-sloping plateau, the lowest part occupied by Lake Victoria. Within this basic framework, Kenya is divided into the following geographic regions: the Lake Victoria basin, the Rift Valley and associated highlands, the eastern plateau forelands, the semiarid and arid areas of the north and south, and the coast.

The semiarid and arid areas in the north and northeast are part of a vast region extending from the Ugandan border through Lake Rudolf to the plateau area between the Ethiopian and Kenyan highlands.

Lava deposits in the Lake Victoria basin have produced fertile and sandy loam soils in the plateaus north and south of Winam Bay. In contrast, the volcanic pile of Mount Elgon produces highly fertile volcanic soils well known for coffee and tea production. The Rift Valley and associated highlands are composed of fertile dark brown loams developed on younger volcanic deposits.

4.2 CLIMATE OF KENYA

The large-scale pressure systems of the western Indian Ocean and adjacent landmasses control seasonal climatic changes. From December to March, northeast winds predominate north of the Equator, while south-to-southeast winds dominate south. These months are fairly dry, although rain may occur locally. The rainy season extends from late March to May, with air flowing from the east in both hemispheres. From June to August, there is little precipitation, and southwest winds prevail north of the Equator as southeast winds prevail in the south.

Plant and animal life

In the highlands between 7,000 and 9,000 feet (2,100 and 2,700 meters), the characteristic landscape consists of patches of evergreen forest separated by vast expanses of short grass. Where the forest has survived human encroachment, it includes economically valuable trees such as cedar (Juniperus procera) and varieties of podo. Above the forest, a zone of bamboo extends to about 10,000 feet (3,000 meters), beyond which there is mountain moorland bearing tree heaths, tree groundsel (a foundation timber of the genus Senecio), and giant lobelia (a widely distributed herbaceous plant). Forests give way to low trees scattered through an even cover of short grass, east and west of the highlands.

Semidesert regions below 3,000 feet (900 metres) give rise to baobab trees. In still drier areas of the north, desert scrub occurs, exposing the bare ground. The vegetation of the coastal region is savanna with patches of residual forests. Almost one-third of Kenya, particularly the western regions and the coastal belt, is infested with tsetse flies and mosquitoes, which are responsible for the spread of, respectively, sleeping sickness (trypanosomiasis) and malaria.

The Famous Baobab Tree Source: amoils.com

Kenya's abundant wildlife population lives mostly outside the country's numerous national parks and game reserves. Baboons and zebras can be found, for instance, along the Nairobi-Nakuru highway, close to human settlements and urban centres. This has created conflict between people and animals that sometimes has been resolved by relocating animals to areas where the human population is less dense. To ameliorate the problem, a "parks beyond parks" program was introduced in the mid-1990s by the Kenya Wildlife Service. The plan has attempted to draw local communities into managing and distributing the income derived from wild animals, thus making people more tolerant of the animals' presence. The program has been somewhat successful, and with community involvement, incidents of poaching in the national parks and game reserves have declined.

Bushbuck, colobus monkeys, and galagos (bush babies) are occasionally found. The bamboo zone contains varieties of duiker and some species of birds, and Highland predators include lions, leopards, and wildcats.

CHAPTER 5
EUROPEAN AND ARAB INFLUENCE ON KENYA

THE PORTUGUESE WERE the first Europeans to explore the region of current-day Kenya: Vasco da Gama visited Mombasa in April 1498.

Da Gama route around Africa

Vasco da Gama set sail from Lisbon, Portugal, in July 1497 to find a direct sea route to India, bypassing the dangerous land routes dominated by Arab and Venetian traders. Da Gama's journey was challenging and perilous, and his fleet faced treacherous weather, navigation difficulties, and tensions with local rulers and traders along the way from North to South Africa.

However, after nearly a year of sailing, Da Gama and his crew visited Mombasa in April 1498 and reached the Calicut port on the Malabar Coast of southwestern India in May 1498.

The voyage marked a significant milestone in the Age of Exploration and established a maritime route between Europe and Asia. Da Gama's expedition was a pivotal moment in world history: it initiated direct maritime Portuguese trade links with South Asia, thus challenging older trading networks over mixed land and sea routes, such as the spice-trade routes that utilised the Persian Gulf, Red Sea and caravans to reach the eastern Mediterranean. The voyage opened up a new trade, cultural exchange, and colonization possibilities.

The new route became important, especially after the Ottoman Turks captured Constantinople in 1453. Turkish control of the eastern Mediterranean inhibited the use of traditional land routes between Europe and India. The new route bypassed Ottoman's political, monopolistic and tariff barriers. It opened up direct trade between Europe and India, allowing for exchanging goods such as spices, textiles, and precious metals. This discovery of a sea route to India contributed to the Portuguese domination of the spice trade and enhanced their influence in the region.

The successful completion of Da Gama's voyage marked the beginning of European slavery in Africa and colonialism in India. It also set the stage for future European powers to establish colonies and trade networks throughout the Indian subcontinent, sparking further exploration and maritime endeavours. It inspired subsequent European explorers, such as Christopher Columbus, Ferdinand Magellan, and others, to embark on their own voyages in search of new trade routes and territories.

Portuguese rule in East Africa focused mainly on a coastal strip in Mombasa. They could not establish colonies inside Africa because of the health threat posed by malaria and yellow fever in the heart of Africa. Only one in ten Europeans survived malaria and yellow fever in Africa. During this period, the Europeans called Africa the "White Man's Grave." However, the discovery of quinine against malaria allowed the Portuguese to move inside and settle down within the continent eventually. The Portuguese presence in East Africa served the purpose of controlling trade within the Indian Ocean and securing the sea routes linking Europe and Asia. Portuguese naval vessels disrupted the commerce of Portugal's enemies within the western Indian Ocean. The Portuguese constructed Fort Jesus in Mombasa in 1593 and demanded high tariffs on items transported through the area, given their strategic control of ports and shipping lanes.

The Omani Arabs besieged Portuguese fortresses and captured Fort Jesus in 1698. Under Seyyid Said (ruled 1807–1856), the Omani sultan moved his capital to Zanzibar in 1824, and the Arabs set up long-distance trade routes into the African interior. Arab, Shirazi and coastal African cultures produced an Islamic Swahili people trading in a variety of up-country commodities, including slaves. The creation of large clove and spice plantations led to the intensification of the slave trade. The slave trade began to grow exponentially at the end of the 17th century with a large slave market based at Zanzibar. Slaves were sourced from the hinterland. Slave caravan routes into the interior of Kenya reached as far as the foothills of Mount Kenya, Lake Victoria and past Lake Baringo into Samburu country.

Arab governance of all the major ports along the East African coast continued until the British secured their 'Indian Jewel'. By the late 19th century, the slave trade on the open seas had been completely strangled by the British. The peak of the slave planta-tion economy in East Africa was between 1875 – 1884. It is esti-mated that between 43,000 – 47,000, slaves were present on the

Kenyan coast. Despite pressure from the British to stop the East African slave trade, it persisted into the early 20th century.

British rule (1895–1963)

The Europeans took over Africa during the 1884 Berlin Conference as part of the agreements. The British were given control over most of the East African coast. The British colonial presence in Kenya began in the late 19th century as part of a trend of seizure of territory across the African continent by European nations that became known as the "Scramble for Africa". Kenya had previously been under the control of the Sultan of Zanzibar, but pressure from Britain and its military had forced the Sultan to hand over the territory to the British Empire.

However, during the Berlin Conference, the Europeans drew the partitioning lines mainly for the Europeans' economic benefit. They did not try to consider any ethnic groups and where their boundaries might start or finish. British Prime Minister Lord Salisbury duly captured the arbitrariness of the partitioning exercise. He said: "We have been engaged in drawing lines on maps of a continent where no white man's feet have ever trod. We have been giving away to ourselves mountains and rivers and lakes, only hindered by the small impediment that we never knew exactly where the mountains and rivers and lakes were.".

However, the partitions were enforced as the national boundaries of Africa throughout the colonisation period, and most of the partitions persisted long after the colonial powers left Africa.

In 1895 the British government took over and claimed the interior as far west as Lake Naivasha; it set up the East Africa Protectorate. With the beginning of colonial rule in 1895, the Rift Valley and the surrounding Highlands, this area's fertile land, became reserved for whites. The whites engaged in large-scale coffee farming, dependent mainly on Kikuyu labour. The colonial takeover occasionally met with some strong local resistance:

Waiyaki wa Hinga

Waiyaki wa Hinga was a prominent Kikuyu chief who lived in what is now Kenya during the late 18th and early 19th centuries. He was born into the Hinga clan of the Kikuyu people, who were one of the largest ethnic groups in pre-colonial Kenya. Waiyaki was known for his bravery, wisdom, and leadership skills, which helped him to become a respected chief among his people.

During his lifetime, the Kikuyu people faced several challenges, including internal conflicts, inter-tribal warfare, and the threat of invasion from neighbouring communities. Waiyaki played a key role in mediating these conflicts and promoting unity among the Kikuyu people.

One of the most significant events in Waiyaki's life was his encounter with the British colonial authorities. In 1895, a British expedition led by Captain F. D. Lugard arrived in Kikuyu territory, seeking to establish British control over the region. Waiyaki initially welcomed the British as potential allies, signed a treaty with Frederick Lugard, and gave him land at Kihumo to build a fort.

But he soon realised they intended to dominate and exploit the Kikuyu people. Immediately after Lugard departed on November 1, 1890, for Mengo, Uganda, British armies and porters at the fort started invading local farms, looting food, and sexually molesting women, heightening hostilities. During one attack in 1891, five people in the garrison were killed. The Kikuyu, too, suffered some casualties. George Wilson, who had been left in charge, fearing more reprisals, evacuated the fort at night after running out of ammunition. When Waiyaki and his men raided the place a few hours later, they found it empty, and in anger, they overran the fort and destroyed the supplies.

An expedition led by Major Eric Smith returned to Dagoretti in April 1891. Armed with 200 rifles, the army raided Waiyaki's village, where 30 villagers were killed. Crops were destroyed and 50 goats were impounded. Waiyaki was captured and disarmed, and a gun barrel was used to inflict a wound on his scalp. As Waiyaki was being taken to Mombasa for trial by Major H. H. Austin, the scalp wound worsened; he died at Kibwezi and was allegedly buried in the mission graveyard. His death was a major blow to the Kikuyu people, who regarded him as a hero and a symbol of resistance against colonial oppression.

Despite his untimely death, Waiyaki's legacy lived among the Kikuyu people. He was remembered as a wise and just leader who fought tirelessly to protect his people's interests. Today, Waiyaki is still revered as a hero and a symbol of the Kikuyu people's struggle for freedom and self-determination.

5.1 BRITISH EAST AFRICA COMPANY

Following severe financial difficulties, the British government, on 1 July 1895, established direct rule through the East African Protectorate, subsequently opening (1902) the fertile highlands to white settlers.

IMPERIAL PARTITIONS OF EASTERN AFRICA
1881–1925

1. Jubaland (to Italian Somaliland, 1925)
2. Rwanda (to Belgium, 1920)
3. Urundi (to Belgium, 1920)
4. Tanganyika Territory (to Britain, 1920)

Possessions

British   German
French   Italian

Eastern Africa partitioned, c. 1914 Source Britannica

The hinterland of East Africa was divided between Britain and Germany: the British took the area north of a line running from the mouth of the Umba River, opposite Pemba Island, and skirting north of Kilimanjaro to a point where latitude 1° S cut the eastern shore of Lake Victoria; the German sphere, Tanganyika (present-day Tanzania), lay to the south of that line.

Initially, the British government was reluctant to become involved in the administration of East Africa. In 1888, it granted the British East Africa Company a Royal Charter. It authorized it to accept existing and future grants and concessions relevant to the administration and development of the British sphere in that part of the world. However, the British East Africa Company's financial resources were inadequate for any large-scale development of the region. This financial problem was finally resolved in 1895 when the British government made Buganda a protectorate and paid the company £250,000 to surrender its charter to the area that is now Kenya. The East Africa Protectorate was proclaimed, with Sir Arthur Hardinge as the first commissioner.

In 1895, the British government constructed a railway from Mombasa to Kisumu, on Lake Victoria, completed in 1901. A major feat of engineering, the Uganda railway was completed in 1903 and was a decisive event in modernising the area. Some 32,000 workers were imported from India to do the manual labour. Many stayed, as did most of the Indian traders and small business people who saw an opportunity to open up the interior of Kenya. The railway opened the interior to European farmers, missionaries, administrators, and systematic government programmes to attack slavery, witchcraft, disease, and famine. The government encouraged European settlement in the fertile highlands with small African populations to make the railway financially viable. The protectorate was responsible for making the railway profitable, and the export of cash crops seemed to provide the perfect solution for generating revenue. At first, only small areas of land in Kiambu district, which had formerly been occupied by Africans and which the Kikuyu regarded as part of their legitimate area of expansion, were allocated to European settlers, but by 1906 more than 1,550 square miles (4,000 square km) had been leased or sold. Some Africans, such as the Maasai, were confined to reserves; by 1911, the Maasai reserve extended south of the railway to the present-day border with Tanzania.

More Africans became separated from their land, and as more European settlers entered the region, the Europeans became concerned with maintaining an adequate supply of African labour. Because few Africans voluntarily chose to work for Europeans, the settlers wanted the government to institute a system that would compel Africans to offer their services to European farmers.

In summary, the arrival of the British marked the beginning of a long period of colonial rule that had a lasting impact on Kenya's history and development. The impact of Colonial Kenya included:

Land Displacement: The British introduced a land-grabbing policy under which they took over large tracts of land belonging to the local communities and redistributed them to white settlers. This led to the displacement of many Kenyans from their ancestral lands and the loss of their source of livelihood.

Cash Crop Economy: To maximize their profits, the British introduced cash crops such as coffee, tea, and sisal to Kenya, which replaced traditional subsistence agriculture as the mainstay of the economy. This led to the exploitation of local labour and the concentration of land ownership in the hands of a few.

Racial Segregation: The British imposed a system of racial segregation under which different races were granted different rights and privileges. The white minority enjoyed superior rights and privileges, while the African majority faced discrimination and oppression. Africans were excluded from political power and denied access to basic services such as education and healthcare.

Mau Mau Uprising: The Mau Mau Uprising was a militant campaign by Kenyan nationalists against British colonial rule in the 1950s. The Mau Mau Uprising was a turning point in the struggle for independence, which Kenya gained in 1963.

The British constructed the Kenya-Uganda Railway, also known as the "Lunatic Express," which was a significant infrastructure project connecting Kenya to the interior of East Africa. The railway was built using forced labour, with many Kenyans dying during its construction, and many communities who lived along its path were displaced.

The traditional leaders of the various Kenyan communities, such as chiefs and elders, were replaced by British-appointed chiefs loyal to the colonial government. The British also introduced a system of taxation that was used to extract resources from the local communities.

5.2 KOITALEL ARAP SAMOEI

In building the railway, the British confronted solid local opposition, especially from Koitalel Arap Samoei, who held the dual roles of chief spiritual and military leader and had the authority to make decisions regarding security matters, particularly waging war and negotiating for peace. Arap Samoei was the supreme chief of the Nandi people of Kenya. He led the Nandi resistance against British colonial rule and prophesied that a black snake would tear through Nandi land, spitting fire, which was seen later as the railway line.

For ten years, he fought against the railway line and train builders. To end the resistance, intelligence officer Richard Meinertzhagen invited Koitalel to a peace truce meeting after leading a rebellion against the colonial invasion of the Nandi. The peace meeting was to be held at 11:00 AM on Thursday, October 19, 1905. Suspecting that he would be killed as his father Kimnyole had foretold,

Samoei instructed Meinertzhagen to come with five companions to meet him at Ketbarak. Samoei was to come with five foretellers.

Contrary to the agreement, Meinertzhagen marched from the fort at Kaptumo with 80 armed men, 75 of whom hid near the meeting venue. It is reported that when Koitalel stretched out his hand to shake it with Meinertzhagen's, Koitalel was killed with a shot at point-blank range. Afterwards, the British decapitated Koitalel's body and took his head to London as proof of his death and a macabre trophy of colonialism. This precipitated the end of the Nandi Resistance. Koitalel has been immortalised as a national hero and a legendary leader in the Kalenjin community.

In 1907, the white settlers were partly allowed a voice in government through the legislative council, a European organisation to which some were appointed, and others elected. But since most of the powers remained in the hands of the Governor, the settlers started lobbying to transform Kenya into a Crown Colony, which meant more powers for the settlers. They obtained this goal in 1920, making the Council more representative of European settlers. Still, Africans were excluded from direct political participation until 1944, when the first one was admitted to the council.

5.3 WORLD WAR I AND ITS AFTERMATH

Germany had hoped that no battles with Britain would be fought on African soil during World War I, but Britain was concerned with its communications with India and the safety of the Ugandan railway. Britain initiated hostilities, to which Germany responded, with Britain ultimately prevailing in East Africa. The conflict caused significant hardships for the African population. Thousands of Africans were forced to serve as porters and soldiers, often with disastrous results, and many Africans died, mostly from disease. The entire East African economic structure was affected, as food production became geared solely toward supplying the troops. This food production fell largely on African women, who did most of the farming. Women were forced to use the same plots of land repeatedly, thereby depleting the soil, because most able-bodied men, who were responsible for clearing new land, had been conscripted. Droughts and famines recurred.

Most of the European settlers quickly joined the armed forces; they left their farms to be looked after by their wives, or else the farms were abandoned. An attempt was made immediately after the war to revive the settler sector by introducing a "soldier settler" scheme, but the hopes of prosperity encouraged by the postwar demand for agricultural products received a severe setback in the early 1920s when a worldwide economic recession brought bankruptcy to many of those who had started out with inadequate capital or had relied on credit from the banks. Stability was further delayed by the replacement of the rupee currency with East African shillings. By the mid-1920s, Kenya's economy had wholly revived, although the Great Depression of the 1930s brought further economic difficulties to East Africa.

5.4 THE UGANDA SCHEME IN KENYA

The Uganda Scheme, also known as the Uganda Proposal, was an idea to create a Jewish homeland in Kenya, East Africa, during the late 19th and early 20th centuries. The proposal was a controversial one that generated significant debate within the Jewish community and beyond.

The idea was presented at the Sixth World Zionist Congress in Basel in 1903 by Theodor Herzl, the founder of the modern Zionist movement. He presented it as a temporary refuge for Jews to escape rising antisemitism in Europe. Theodor Herzl, the founder of modern political Zionism, had advocated for a Jewish homeland in Palestine for several years. However, as negotiations with the Ottoman Empire over the possibility of establishing a Jewish state in Palestine stalled, Herzl began to explore other options.

British Colonial Secretary Joseph Chamberlain was aware of the ambitions of the Zionist Organisation to create a Jewish homeland. During his trip, Chamberlain suggested, "If Dr Herzl were inclined to transfer his efforts to East Africa, there would be no difficulty in finding land in Kenya suitable for Jewish settlers."

Herzl was later introduced to Chamberlain by Israel Zangwill in the spring of 1903, a few weeks after the Kishinev massacre of Jews in Moldova in 1903. A second massacre erupted in October 1905, leading to 49 Jews killed, over 592 injured, several Jewish women raped, and 1,500 homes damaged. American Jews started a large-scale organization of financial help and assisted with the emigration of Jews to America. The incident also focused world-wide attention on the persecution of Jews in Russia and led Theodor Herzl to propose the Uganda Scheme as a temporary refuge for the Jews.

The British government was motivated by a desire to solve the problem of Jewish immigration to Palestine, which was causing tension with the Arab population. At the same time, the British also hoped to secure a strategic foothold in East Africa, which was seen as a crucial region for trade and commerce.

Chamberlain offered 13,000 square kilometres (5,000 sq mi) at Uasin Gishu, an isolated area atop the Mau Escarpment in modern Kenya. The land was considered suitable because of its temperate hill station-like climate and relative isolation, surrounded by the Mau Forest. The offer was to be a temporary refuge from persecution for the Jewish people.

However, the Russian Jewish delegates were particularly unhappy with the plan because they thought that it would divert attention and resources away from the goal of creating a Jewish homeland in Palestine. They also saw the Uganda Scheme as a compromise that would dilute the Zionist movement's original vision. In addition, there were concerns about the suitability of the proposed land in Kenya for Jewish settlement. Some argued that the region was unsuitable for agriculture and that the climate was inhospitable, and the original Kenyan people in the area were warlike and would not tolerate such an incursion.

One of the critics of the Uganda Project was Chaim Weizmann, a prominent Zionist leader, who argued that the Jewish people had a historical and religious connection to Palestine that could not be replicated in Kenya. Weizmann believed that the Jewish people should continue focusing on establishing a homeland in Palestine.

In 1908, at the Eighth Zionist Congress, the Uganda Scheme was officially rejected in favour of the continued pursuit of a Jewish homeland in Palestine.

In his essay "What If the Jewish State Had Been Established in East Africa, " Adam Rovner argues that the Uganda project could have dramatically altered the course of Jewish and African history. And it is impossible to know how this would have affected the Kenyans and the development of Zionism and the state of Israel.

Lavie Tidhar's novel "Unholy Land" challenges readers to think deeply about our world and the paths not taken. It is a powerful reminder that the past is never truly gone, and our choices today will shape tomorrow's world.

5.5 KENYAN PROTEST TOWARDS INDEPENDENCE

In 1923, the colonial government began to concern itself with the plight of the African peoples; the colonial secretary issued a White Paper in which he indicated that African interests in the colony had to be paramount. One area that needed improvement was education for Africans; up to that, they could do basic administration jobs, nearly all African schooling had been provided by missionaries.

As more Africans worked on European farms and in urban areas such as Nairobi, they began to imitate political techniques used by

European settlers as they attempted to gain more direct representation in colonial politics. At the outset, political pressure groups developed along ethnic lines, the first one being the Young Kikuyu Association (later the East African Association), established in 1921, with Harry Thuku as its first president. Throughout the 1920s and '30s European settlers continued to oppose African demands for greater representation on the Legislative Council.

THE MAU MAU UPRISING

The Mau Mau uprising began in 1952 as a reaction to inequalities and injustices in British-controlled Kenya. From around 1890, the British began to move inland, hoping to gain access to the fertile highlands and provide greater security. A railway line from Mombasa to Kisumu was built using Indian workers, and British forces were sent to suppress any resistance from the ethnic groups living in the central highlands – predominantly the Maasai, the Kikuyu, and the Kamba. The British displays of force intended to intimidate locals into submission, such as shooting Africans at random, quickly led to the withdrawal of hospitality from those living in the interior.

The arrival of more European settlers in 1903 added to the troubles of the indigenous people. Whilst the numbers of white immigrants were relatively few, they claimed a disproportionately large amount of land, most of which was seized from Africans. A reallocation policy was undertaken, expropriating fertile land from locals for white farmers, who mostly moved from Britain or South Africa. This process began a pattern defining relations between Europeans and indigenous Kenyans for the first half of the 20th century.

The fertile areas were referred to as the "White Highlands" by the British colonialists. Between 1902 and 1961, the colonial government reserved these areas exclusively for Europeans. They included Machakos, Nairobi, Thika, Mt Kenya region, Laikipia,

Naivasha, Nakuru, Kericho, Sotik, Lumbwa, Songhor, Nandi, Uasin Gishu, Trans Nzoia, and Mt Elgon.

In his book "Kenya: A History Since Independence," Charles Hornsby explains that many of the first settlers came from the British aristocracy and military, accustomed to command and with deeply engrained prejudices against foreigners. "These imperial settlers were convinced that they were the natural rulers of Kenya (as of everywhere else) and that Africans were their feudal subjects. Colonialization displaced many inhabitants in the "White Highlands", while others sold their parcels while assuming they were merely ceding the use of the land.

Maasai is one of the few Kenya tribes that did not really resist the British.This was because 30 years before the arrival of the British colonialists, the Maasai had suffered drought, wars, and outbreaks of smallpox and rinderpest, which depopulated their land in Central Rift Valley and killed most of their cattle. They thus gave in to the colonialists and even became mercenaries for the British alongside the Kamba and the Luhya Wanga. The Maasai lost the entire Central Rift Valley. The British also signed controversial land agreements with the Maasai, most of whom were illiterate, alienating them from colonial settlements. One of these agreements was the infamous Maasai Agreement of August 1904, a treaty signed by the colonial government and Maasai elders. The Maasai ceded possession of pastures in the Central Rift Valley in return for exclusive rights to a southern reserve in Kajiado and a northern reserve in Laikipia.

Therefore, when Kenya became independent in 1963, there was hope among the inhabitants, particularly those who had fought against the colonialists, that they would get their land back.

However, during the negotiations for Kenya's independence, Kenyatta accepted the colonialists' demands that the White settlers remain on their farms if they wished to. That land was to be transferred only on the basis of "willing buyer, willing seller".

While the Maasai generally avoided military confrontation with the British, the Kikuyu attempted to mount some resistance to the intrusion of imperial forces into their land. This resistance was met with brutality from the British, who carried out executions and punitive expeditions to hunt down Kikuyu and Kamba people. The British also used these actions to elevate collaborators – Africans willing to cooperate with the British – to positions of power. This campaign, combined with the famine and disease that swept the region during this period, resulted in significant loss of life and property amongst the indigenous people. Also, an epidemic of rinderpest brought in by the European livestock, a disease that severely affected native livestock, heavily contributed to the devastation of the local population.

In Towett J. Kimaiyo's book, "Ogiek Land Cases and Historical Injustices 1902 – 2004," he states that Kenya was declared a British Protectorate on 15 June 1895, which conferred to the British Crown political jurisdiction over the land from the Coast to the Rift Valley.

In 1901, the East African (Lands) ordinance-in-council was enacted, conferring to the Commissioner of the Protectorate the right to sell up to 1,000 acres of Crown land in freehold to any person as grant leases of 99 years; the 99 year-duration was extended to 999 years in 1915. As a result, between 1902 and 1915, about 7.5 million acres—20% of Kenya's best and most fertile land —were reserved for the settlers as Crown Property.

The Crown Lands Ordinance Act enacted by the British in 1915 removed the few remaining land rights of the native people, completing a process that essentially transformed them into an agricultural working class, dispossessed of their land. The influx of settlers increased sharply after the end of the First World War, as the British government undertook a scheme to settle many ex-soldiers in the region. Continuing land seizures by the British to provide for these settlers drove Africans to form organisations that campaigned for greater land rights for the indigenous inhabitants. These organisations included the East African Association (EAA), formed in 1921 but banned the following year, and the Kenyan African Union (KAU), formed in 1942.

Kenyans ' discontent was intensified after the Second World War ended by the lack of progress. Hundreds of thousands of Kenyans lived in poverty in the slums around Nairobi, with little chance of employment or basic social justice. In comparison, most white Europeans and many Indians who had settled in Nairobi enjoyed a conspicuous level of wealth and frequently treated indigenous Africans with hostility and contempt. A similar state of affairs existed in rural areas, where 3000 European families owned more land than the one million Kikuyu driven into reserves. This situation, the culmination of decades of mistreatment and oppression under British rule, created an atmosphere of discontentment that fed into the various Kenyan nationalist movements and ultimately led to the Mau Mau uprising.

Mau Mau Emerges

By the early fifties, the younger, more radical elements of the nationalist movement in Kenya had begun to split away from those campaigning for constitutional reform. These Africans were generally Kikuyu who had been reduced to squatters on their own land by the laws introduced by the British and were increasingly disillusioned with the conservative change espoused by organisations like the KAU. Instead, they were prepared to resort to force to achieve their aims, and in the years preceding the uprising, they carried out small-scale attacks and sabotaged European property. These militant activists quickly consolidated their support throughout the Kenyan highlands, using a campaign of oath-taking to commit others to the anti-colonial cause. The movement that emerged became known as the Mau Mau. As the Mau Mau movement grew, more moderate elements among the Kenyans were swept aside by popular pressure.

Despite awareness of the movement's growth, the British government and settler communities initially made no concessions aside from a few token measures and instead continued existing policies of repression and even proposed new legislation to reduce the rights of the indigenous people even further. This inflexibility forced the Mau Mau into a period of armed resistance. The lack of recognition of the threat posed by the squatter movement demonstrated how the Europeans did not consider Kenyan nationalists capable of organising significant opposition to the colonial regime.

Those initially targeted by the Mau Mau were Kikuyu, who collaborated with the Europeans. In 1952 a wave of violence was directed at police witnesses who provided testimony against Africans, particularly in cases related to the Mau Mau. Prominent collaborators were assassinated, and many white settlers were also attacked. Police responded by initiating a mass campaign of arrests, arresting Kikuyu suspected of Mau Mau involvement, and taking others into preventative detention to neutralise the Mau Mau support base. However, this indiscriminate repression had the opposite effect of what was intended and drove many more indigenous Kenyans to support the movement. By mid-1952, around 90% of Kikuyu adults had taken the Mau Mau oath.

The government encouraged Kikuyu chiefs to speak out against Mau Mau and administer 'cleansing oaths', supposedly absolving Kenyans from the oaths taken to support the anti-colonial cause. KAU officials, including Jomo Kenyatta, also publically spoke out against the movement's actions, although many stopped short of outright condemnation. In October 1952, Senior Chief Waruhiu, a prominent collaborator and the harshest critic of the Mau Mau among the Kikuyu chiefs, was assassinated near Nairobi. His death prompted celebration amongst Mau Mau supporters and consternation in government. The colonial administration finally realised that the Mau Mau posed a severe threat to colonial rule in Kenya, and the decision was taken to actively challenge and engage the rebels. Two weeks after Waruhiu's death, the government declared a State of Emergency.

The Uprising

The Declaration of Emergency was accompanied by Operation Jock Scott, a coordinated police operation that arrested 187 Kikuyu, who the government considered leaders of the Mau Mau movement. Along with the deployment of British troops, this was hoped to disrupt and intimidate the rebels into submission. Mau Mau supporters responded by assassinating another senior Kikuyu chief and several white settlers. Thousands of Mau Mau left their homes and set up camp in the forests of the Aberdares and Mt. Kenya, creating a base of resistance to the government. These fighters soon began to organise, and several military commanders emerged, including Waruhiu Itote and Dedan Kimathi.

Hostilities were relatively subdued for the remainder of 1952, but the following year began with a series of violent killings of European farmers and loyalist Africans. This sufficiently shocked the white population into demanding that the government take more action to combat the Mau Mau, and so the Kenyan security forces were placed under the command of the British Army and began to surround the Mau Mau strongholds in the forests. This was accompanied by large-scale eviction of Kikuyu squatters from land that had been selected for European settlers. The government troops adopted a policy of collective punishment, which was again intended to undermine popular support of the Mau Mau. Under this policy, if a village member was found to be a Mau Mau supporter, the entire village was treated as such. This led to the eviction of many Kikuyu, who were forced to abandon their homes and possessions and sent to areas designated as Kikuyu reserves. A particularly unpleasant element of the eviction policy was the use of concentration camps to process those suspected of Mau Mau involvement. Abuse and torture were commonplace in these camps, as British guards used beatings, sexual abuse, and executions to extract information from prisoners and to force them to renounce their allegiance to the anti-colonial cause. Mass evictions furthered anger and fear among the Kikuyu, who had already suffered through decades of land reallocation and drove hundreds of squatters to join the Mau Mau fighters in the forest.

A British Prison camp in Kenya, 1954. Source: Getty Images

The British built a network of concentration camps across the colony to hold suspected rebels to facilitate the interrogations. They divided internees into three classes according to their degree of perceived cooperation. In time, the camps expanded to hold hundreds of thousands of Kikuyu. One day in Nairobi, the British arrested 130,000 men and shipped them off to the camps, while another 170,000 women and children were sent to the reservations. Even some "loyal" Kikuyu were herded into the camps as the British policy seemed to shift into full-scale genocide.

At the British concentration camp in Kenya Source Getty Images

Very little food made it to the prisoners in these camps, and hunger-related disease was rife. The beating of suspects to obtain evidence was rampant, especially in Nairobi. The favoured inter-rogation method used by a British soldier was to hold a man upside down with his head in a bucket of water and ram sand into his rectum. Men were raped with knives, snakes, and scorpions to spread fear, while women were gang-raped or had their breasts mutilated with pliers.

A former white settler member of the Kenya Regiment explained: "We would go and pick up a few of the filthy pigs and bring them to one of the interrogation centres set up by the CID. We would give them a good thrashing, which would be a bloody awful mess by the time we were done. I never knew that a Kikuyu had so many brains until we cracked open a few heads."

Some victims' skin was burnt off, and they were forced to eat their own castrated testicles. One particular Kikuyu man was slowly electrocuted to death, his testicles and ears already cut off while one eyeball hung out of its socket. Fighters were tied to the backs of Land Rovers and driven around the village to slow and painful deaths. Men and women were made to run around with toilet buckets on their heads and sometimes made to eat the excrement in the buckets. Sometimes men would be forced to carry the decomposing bodies of killed insurgents unearthed by the British officers. Some were swung around and around by their hair, while others held their necks and their heads banged together until they were unconscious. Pepper and water mixtures were sometimes poured into the vaginas of groaning and vomiting women.

Among the detainees who suffered severe mistreatment was Hussein Onyango Obama, the grandfather of Barack Obama, the former President of the United States. According to his widow, British soldiers forced pins into his fingernails and buttocks and squeezed his testicles between metal rods; two others were castrated.

The historian Robert Edgerton describes the methods used during the emergency:

> "If a question was not answered to the interrogator's satisfaction, the subject was beaten and kicked. More force was applied if that did not lead to the desired confession, and it rarely did. Electric shock was widely used, and so was the fire. Women were choked and held under water; gun barrels, beer bottles, and even knives were thrust into their vaginas. Men had beer bottles thrust up their rectums. Some police officers did not bother with more time-consuming forms of torture; they simply shot any suspect who refused to answer and then told the next suspect to dig his own grave. When the grave was finished, the man was asked if he would now be willing to talk."

ROBERT EDGERTON

"Electric shock and cigarettes and fire were widely used. Bottles (often broken), gun barrels, knives, snakes, vermin, and hot eggs were thrust up men's rectums and women's vaginas. The screening teams whipped, shot, burned and mutilated Mau Mau suspects, ostensibly to gather intelligence for military operations and as court evidence".

CAROLINE ELKINS

Outside of the camps, reservations, and "villages," the colonial government had resorted to open violence and routinely displayed the corpses of executed prisoners at crossroads as a warning. In 18 months, RAF Lincoln bombers dropped over 6 million bombs into Kenya's forests to disrupt guerrilla activity. After one gruesome massacre, the RAF dusted Kikuyu areas with photographs of mutilated women to intimidate the populace.

The ironic fact is that Kikuyu genocide took place in the 1950s, a decade after the Holocaust and the West's promise never again to allow the destruction of entire peoples. It saw virtually the population of 1.5 million Kikuyu locked up in concentration camps, where they were starved, beaten, and tortured to death by the tens of thousands, and in some centres, most children perished. Tens of thousands of Kenyans were killed by British forces.

The Defeat of the Mau Mau

A series of large-scale engagements between the two sides occurred in 1953, with the underequipped Mau Mau forces suffering heavy losses. By the end of the year, over 30,000 Mau Mau had been confirmed as killed and 1,000 captured, and almost 100,000 alleged Mau Mau supporters had been arrested.

By the end of 1954, one million Kikuyu had been driven from their family homes and rehoused in these villages, which were little more than fenced camps and were prone to famine and disease. These heavy-handed and ruthless strategies employed in Nairobi and the countryside by the British effectively cut off much of the material and logistical support for the forest fighters.

Compared to the vast African loss of life, only 32 European civilian settlers were killed by the Mau Mau; more settlers died in car accidents during this period. 1955 British Prime Minister Winston Churchill authorised the campaign's indefinite continuation.

In 2012, the British Foreign Office was humiliated when it was revealed that Britain systematically destroyed evidence that would have exposed the evil of its imperialist machine to the world.

According to the UK Guardian,

> *"Those papers that survived the purge were flown discreetly to Britain where they were hidden for 50 years in a secret Foreign Office archive, beyond the reach of historians and members of the public, and in breach of legal obligations for them to be transferred into the public domain."*

THE UK GUARDIAN

The papers showed that ministers in London knew the Kikuyu were being tortured and killed in Kenya but chose to remain silent. The paper also showed that Iain Macleod, secretary of state for the colonies, directed that post-independence governments should not get any material that "might embarrass Her Majesty's government". All Britain wanted to do was save face, but the blood of the Kikuyu would tell a different story and escape the labyrinth of British lies and deceit.

The Effect of the Mau Mau on the Independence Struggle

Despite the defeat of the Mau Mau, the uprising had put Kenya on an inevitable path to independence from colonial rule. There were several reasons for this. The first was that it was made clear to the Kenyan population that the Europeans were far from invincible and that their rule was more tenuous than previously realised. Consequently, the effective resistance to the colonial rule shown by Mau Mau accelerated the pace of nationalism in Kenya and throughout East Africa. The actions of the white settler community had demonstrated how fearful they were of indigenous opposition to their land seizures, and divisions emerged between extremists and moderates, weakening the political domination the community previously enjoyed. In addition, the government's brutality had effectively driven a fresh wave of anti-colonialist sentiment in the country.

Also important was the financial impact of the Mau Mau uprising. The British were forced to spend a tremendous amount of money to combat the rebels, and with the lackluster British economy still suffering from the effects of the Second World War, this expenditure doubtless sapped the British's will to continue maintaining their colonial ambitions in the face of such determined opposition. In addition, the organised approach taken by the Mau Mau and the difficulties they posed for British troops challenged European assertions that Kenyan nationalists were incapable of effectively challenging colonial rule.

Perhaps the greatest impact that the Mau Mau uprising had on the struggle for Kenya's independence was its role in politicising and mobilising the agrarian sectors and shaping their political awareness and economic thinking. By awakening this key section of Kenyan society to the damage and repression caused by colonial rule, the Mau Mau set in motion a popular independence movement that captured the national consciousness of the economically disenfranchised Kenyan people like never before.

5.7 WORLD WAR II TO INDEPENDENCE

Kenya's Struggle for Independence is a significant part of the country's history, and it is a story of how people fought against colonialism to gain their freedom and self-determination. The movement's roots for Kenyan independence can be traced back to the late 19th century when European powers began to colonize Africa. The imperial powers saw Africa as a source of raw materials, and they believed that Africans were inferior and needed to be civilized.

The struggle for independence actually began in the 1920s and lasted until 1963, when Kenya finally gained independence. During this period, the Kenyan people experienced a lot of oppression, including forced labour, land alienation, and political marginalization. Various events, including protests, strikes, and armed resistance, marked the struggle for independence.

The British colonial government encouraged the cultivation of cash crops such as coffee, tea, and sisal. This led to the displacement of many Africans from their land and the loss of their traditional way of life. The Africans who were displaced became labourers on European-owned plantations. The harsh working conditions and low wages led to widespread resentment and anger among the African population. The Africans began to realize they were being oppressed and exploited by the European powers, and they began to organize themselves into political parties and movements to demand their rights. The first political party was the East Africa Association, founded in 1919 by Harry Thuku. The party's main objective was to demand political representation for Africans and to challenge the British colonial government's policies.

The outbreak of World War II also forced the colony to focus on its borders; with the entry of Italy into the war, Kenya's northern border with Ethiopia and Somaliland was briefly threatened.

The colonial government then turned its attention to African political representation, and in 1944 Kenya became the first East African territory to include an African on its Legislative Council.

The number was increased to two in 1946, four in 1948, and eight in 1951, although the governor appointed all representatives from a list of names submitted by local governments. This, however, did not satisfy African demands for political equality. The Mau Mau Rebellion occurred between 1952 and 1960 and was significant in Kenya's struggle for independence. The Mau Mau rebellion was a turning point in Kenya's struggle for independence, as it brought international attention to the country's plight and forced the British to consider granting independence.

Negotiations with British officials were another critical stage in Kenya's struggle for independence. In the early 1960s, a series of talks took place between Kenyan leaders and British officials. These negotiations resulted in the Lancaster House Agreement, which granted Kenya independence on December 12, 1963. The Lancaster House Conference was a series of negotiations between the British government, led by Secretary of State for the Colonies Duncan Sandys, and representatives of various Kenyan political groups. The discussions aimed to resolve the political deadlock between Kenya's main nationalist party, the Kenya African National Union (KANU), and the British colonial administration. The agreement also established the framework for a new constitution and the formation of political parties. The negotiations were marked by compromise and political manoeuvring as both sides sought to achieve their goals while avoiding violence and instability.

However, the Lancaster House Agreement was not without controversy. The negotiations were primarily focused on political power-sharing between ethnic groups and political parties, often overshadowing discussions on economic and social issues. Land redistribution, one of the key concerns of Kenyan nationalists, was not adequately addressed, leading to ongoing land disputes and inequalities that still persist in Kenya today.

The formation of political parties was the final stage in Kenya's struggle for independence. Several political parties emerged in the years leading up to independence, including the Kenya African National Union (KANU) and the Kenya African Democratic Union (KADU). These parties were formed to represent the various ethnic groups in Kenya and to compete for power in the new government. KANU emerged as the dominant party, with Jomo Kenyatta as its leader. Kenyatta became Kenya's first president and played a significant role in shaping the country's future. The formation of political parties was a critical step in Kenya's transition to independence, as it allowed for peaceful competition and the establishment of a democratic government.

The Kenya African National Union (KANU), founded in May of that year and favouring a strong centralized government, was built around Kenyatta. The negotiations at Lancaster House involved leaders of various political parties, such as Jomo Kenyatta, the head of KANU, and Ronald Ngala, the head of KADU. They discussed issues such as the transfer of power, the distribution of land and resources, and the protection of minority rights. However, disagreements and tensions, especially between KANU and KADU, threatened to derail the talks. Finally, with the help of mediator Lord Gore-Booth, a compromise was reached that satisfied most parties and paved the way for independence.

A coalition government of the two parties was formed in 1962, and after elections in May of 1963, Kenyatta became prime minister under a constitution that gave Kenya self-government. Following further discussions in London, Kenya became fully independent on Dec. 12, 1963. Kenya became a republic (with Kenyatta as its first president and Oginga Odinga as vice president). After independence, KANU established a one-party state and dominated Kenyan politics for several decades.

One of the legacies of Kenya's struggle for independence is the emergence of a strong sense of national identity among the

Kenyan people. The struggle brought together people from different ethnic and linguistic backgrounds who united under the banner of nationalism and shared aspirations for freedom and self-determination. This sense of national identity has been instrumental in shaping Kenya's political landscape and has helped foster a shared sense of purpose and collective action among the country's citizens. The struggle also led to the development of a vibrant civil society committed to promoting democratic values and ensuring accountability among the country's leaders. The struggle created a space for people to mobilize and organize around social and political justice issues, which led to the formation of various civil society organizations that continue to play a crucial role in shaping Kenya's political discourse. The struggle brought attention to economic inequality and exploitation issues, which were prevalent under British colonial rule. After gaining independence, the Kenyan government embarked on a program of economic development that aimed to address these issues and create a more equitable and prosperous society. Although progress has been slow, Kenya has made significant strides in infrastructure development, education, healthcare, roads, railways, airports, and the growth of industries such as tourism and technology. The country's economic growth has helped to create job opportunities and improve the standard of living for many Kenyans.

CHAPTER 6
THE REPUBLIC OF KENYA

President Kenyatta

6.1 KENYATTA'S RULE

KENYA GAINED independence from the British colonialists on December 12, 1963. The reign of President Jomo Kenyatta, the first President of Kenya, elicits both admiration and criticism when critically reflected upon. While he is celebrated as a founding father and a symbol of independence, his leadership and policies also faced significant scrutiny.

Once he became President, Jomo Kenyatta maintained the system of freehold land titles and did not question how the white settlers acquired the land. Individual private ownership rights continued to derive from the president, just as in colonial times.

After independence, most of the good lands in Kenya belonged to the white settlers, and land acquisition from the settlers was largely achieved through four methods: "willing buyer, willing seller", settlement schemes, shirika schemes (cooperative or collective farms), and land-buying companies.

President Jomo Kenyatta's land reform policies and his approach towards addressing the issue of land ownership by white settlers in Kenya have been the subject of criticism and debate. While some argue that his efforts were necessary to address historical injustices and redistribute land to Kenyans, others criticize the implementation and outcomes of these policies.

One main criticism of Kenyatta's land reforms is the slow and insufficient pace of land redistribution. The process of reclaiming land from white settlers and distributing it to landless Kenyans was criticized for being overly cautious and not effectively addressing the deep-seated inequalities in land ownership. Critics argue that the government's reluctance to implement more radical measures hindered the goal of achieving a more equitable distribution of land.

Another point of contention is the compensation provided to white settlers for the land acquired through the land reform process. Some argue that the compensation was excessive and disproportionate, benefiting the former colonizers rather than adequately compensating Kenya's people who had been dispossessed of their land during the colonial period. This has led to accusations of a lack of justice and fairness in the land reform process.

Furthermore, critics argue that the land reforms did not fully address the underlying issues of Kenya's land management and land tenure systems. The focus on redistributing land from white settlers overshadowed the need for comprehensive land governance reforms, including addressing issues such as land corruption, land speculation, and insecure land rights for ordinary citizens.

However, it is important to note that these criticisms should be considered within the historical and political context of the time. President Kenyatta faced numerous challenges, including the need for stability and the delicate task of balancing competing interests within a diverse society. Land reform is a complex and multifaceted issue that requires careful consideration of legal, economic, and social factors. Kenyatta's approach was a delicate balancing act, aiming to address historical injustices while maintaining stability and avoiding the widespread violence during land redistribution in other African countries.

The amounts paid for the acquired land have been viewed as excessive, favouring former colonisers over dispossessed Kenyans. As a result, in the early years of independence, the weight of colonialism was very heavy on Kenya. The British demanded that Kenya spend a large part of her budget to resettle African farmers back on the white British farmers' land. The departing UK government originally initiated the plan as part of ending colonialism. This meant the Kenya government had to pay exorbitantly (50% of the budget) to buy back the land from the European white farmers. Another 22% of the budget was paid towards the administration of this plan. The scheme was called the transfer of land ownership from white Europeans to Africans, nearly bankrupting Kenya. When the country finished paying for this initiative, the government of Kenya only had a modest income left to invest in agriculture.

By the time Kenyatta took over the government, agricultural services were already 'neglected', and the focus on improving agriculture and rural areas was abandoned. Instead, the Kenyan public was presented with education as the centrepiece of national planning, appealing to the popular dream of escaping from farming into a world of desk jobs, 'highly skilled people, and 'modern living' (Republic of Kenya, 1966).

Though Kenya did not completely neglect agriculture to the same extent as other African countries did, it followed a strategy of betting on the rich, deliberately promoting inequality with the vague expectation that the poor would ultimately benefit. Kenya's First National Development Plan explicitly stated that credit would be provided only to a prosperous elite group. The progressive smallholders would benefit from only about 3% of Kenya's land-owning peasantry (excluding pastoralists). The fertiliser was also generously subsidised in Kenya, but only the rich benefited. Money was invested in already large well-to-do farms, those who did not necessarily need the money, rather than in the poor who had the greatest need. Kenyatta allowed politicians and civil servants to buy farms in Uasin Gishu and Trans Nzoia from the Agricultural Development Corporation (ADC), which acquired and continued to buy farms from the settlers, further contributing to inequalities in land ownership.

One of the most significant events of post-independence Kenya was the establishment of a new constitution. The first constitution of Kenya was drafted in 1963, and it provided for a parliamentary system of government with a president as the head of state. The Constitution also established a bill of rights that guaranteed basic freedoms and rights to all citizens. In 1964 Kenyatta sought the help of British troops to suppress a mutiny by the army. In subsequent years, the Constitution was amended several times to reflect changing political and social realities.

Another key feature of post-independence Kenya was the development of a strong, centralized government. Under his leadership, the government pursued policies to promote economic growth, development, and social welfare. The government also invested heavily in education, health, and infrastructure and established various institutions to support these sectors. Despite the significant progress made in post-independence Kenya, the country also faced ethnic and political violence. The country was divided into various ethnic groups, and tensions between these groups sometimes resulted in violence. The government also faced criticism for handling political opposition and allegations of corruption and human rights abuses.

Another point of contention was corruption. Kenyatta's presidency witnessed the emergence of corruption as a systemic problem within the government and bureaucracy. The lack of effective anti-corruption measures and the perceived impunity of high-ranking officials undermined public trust and hindered socio-economic development. Critics argue that Kenyatta's government failed to adequately address this issue, setting the stage for the persistence of corruption in Kenya's subsequent administrations.

However, it is important to acknowledge that Kenyatta's leadership also had notable achievements. He played a crucial role in leading Kenya to independence, fostering a sense of national identity, and establishing a stable foundation for the nation. His government invested in infrastructure development, education, and healthcare, which laid the groundwork for Kenya's subsequent progress.

Despite these challenges, Kenyatta's reign is widely regarded as a crucial period in Kenya's history. His leadership helped to unite the country and lay the foundation for economic and social development. Kenyatta's legacy remains influential in Kenya today, and his political party, the Kenya African National Union (KANU), remains an important force in Kenyan politics.

The question of who should succeed the ageing president exacerbated the disagreements already existing among the country's leaders. The transfer of power took place smoothly from Kenyatta, owing to the skilful leadership of the attorney general, Charles Njonjo, and the minister of finance, Mwai Kibaki, who ensured that, upon Kenyatta's death in August 1978, he was succeeded by his deputy, Daniel Arap Moi, a member of the minority Kalenjin people.

6.2 MOI'S RULE

Daniel Arap Moi ruled Kenya as its second president for 24 years, from 1978 to 2002. His regime was characterized by the Nyayo philosophy, "Nyayo" is a Swahili word that translates to "footsteps," symbolizing the path or track the nation should follow.

The Nyayo philosophy emphasized peace, unity, and development as core principles for Kenya's progress. It aimed to foster a sense of national cohesion and stability, particularly in the aftermath of the country's political upheaval and economic challenges during the 1980s and 1990s.

The philosophy also highlighted the importance of socioeconomic development and progress. It called for self-reliance, entrepreneurship, and collective responsibility in the pursuit of economic growth. President Moi's government implemented various development projects, particularly in infrastructure, education, and healthcare, as part of the Nyayo philosophy's objectives.

Under his leadership, Kenya saw infrastructure development projects, expansion of education, and efforts to enhance agricultural productivity. Moi also maintained relative stability in the region during a period of political turmoil in neighbouring countries.

Moi accomplished some notable achievements during his tenure, particularly in the areas of education and infrastructure. He launched a nationwide campaign to increase literacy rates, and by the time he left office, Kenya had one of the highest literacy rates in Africa. Moi also oversaw the construction of roads, schools, hospitals, and other public works projects, which helped to modernize the country and improve the lives of many Kenyans.

One of the major criticisms of Moi's regime is the erosion of democratic principles and the suppression of political dissent. During his presidency, Moi's government implemented policies restricting freedom of expression, assembly, and association. Opposition parties were stifled, independent media outlets faced censorship, and activists were subjected to harassment and intimidation. This repressive environment undermined the growth of democratic institutions and limited political pluralism in the country.

Furthermore, Moi's regime has been accused of widespread human rights abuses. Reports of extrajudicial killings, arbitrary detentions, and torture were common during his presidency. The Special Branch, Moi's intelligence agency, was notorious for its use of violence and intimidation against political opponents and activists. These human rights violations tarnished Kenya's international reputation and raised concerns about the rule of law and the protection of basic rights and freedoms.

In conclusion, a critical reflection on the reign of President Arap Moi reveals a complex legacy. While he made contributions to infrastructure and social development, his regime was marred by political repression, human rights abuses, and economic misman-agement. The erosion of democratic principles, stifling of dissent, and corruption allegations remain significant concerns. It is essen-tial to learn from the past and strive for a more inclusive, transpar-ent, and accountable governance system that upholds human rights, fosters economic growth, and ensures the well-being of all Kenyans.

Moi announced in 2002 that he would not run again for the presi-dency, and Uhuru Kenyatta, son of Jomo Kenyatta, was chosen to be KANU's presidential candidate. Kibaki soundly defeated Keny-atta in the 2002 presidential elections, thus ending KANU's long uninterrupted rule.

6.3 KIBAKI'S RULE

Mwai Kibaki served as the third president of Kenya from 2002 to 2013. His tenure was marked by a mix of successes and challenges, including significant economic growth, political reforms, and continuing issues with corruption and ethnic tensions.

Kibaki inherited a deeply divided country plagued by corruption, poverty, and a lack of basic services. He faced high expectations from Kenyans and the international community to address these issues and turn the country around.

Although Kibaki pledged to fight the corruption that had plagued Kenya under KANU's rule, it continued to affect the country's economic and political credibility in the 21st century.

One of Kibaki's most significant achievements was his successful management of the Kenyan economy. During his tenure, Kenya experienced a period of sustained economic growth, with the GDP increasing by an average of 6% per year. Kibaki pursued policies to attract foreign investment and improve infrastructure, which helped create jobs and boost the country's overall economic prospects.

Kibaki also initiated a number of important political reforms during his presidency. He oversaw the creation of a new constitution in 2010, which significantly devolved power from the central government to local authorities and improved protections for human rights. Kibaki also established the National Accord and Reconciliation Act, which helped to quell ethnic tensions and political violence following the disputed 2007 presidential election.

Despite these successes, Kibaki's presidency was also marked by significant challenges. Corruption remained a major problem, and several high-profile corruption scandals rocked his administration. Kibaki was criticized for not doing enough to tackle corruption, and his government faced widespread allegations of nepotism and cronyism.

In 2005 his administration was embroiled in a corruption scandal, and later that year, a draft of a new constitution championed by

Kibaki was defeated in a national referendum. Kibaki also faced criticism for handling ethnic tensions, particularly in the aftermath of the 2007 presidential election. The election was marred by violence that claimed over 1,000 lives, and Kibaki's government was accused of failing to address the underlying causes of the violence.

December 2007 Election

The 2007 presidential election in Kenya was one of the most contentious and violent one in the country's history. The election was marred by allegations of rigging and irregularities, which led to widespread protests, violence, and, ultimately, a disputed outcome.

The main contenders in the presidential race were the incumbent President Mwai Kibaki of the Party of National Unity (PNU) and Raila Odinga of the Orange Democratic Movement (ODM). The election was highly anticipated, with both candidates enjoying significant support bases.

The election boasted a record-high voter turnout and was one of the closest in Kenya's history. The provisional results indicated that Odinga would be victorious, but, when the final election results were released after a delay, Kibaki was declared the winner by a narrow margin. Odinga immediately disputed the outcome, and international observers questioned the validity of the final results. There were also allegations of vote-rigging and other irregularities, which led to a breakdown of trust in the electoral process.

Widespread protests ensued throughout the country and degenerated into horrific acts of violence involving some of Kenya's many ethnic groups, most notable of which were the Kikuyu (Kibaki's group), the Kalenjin, and the Luo (Odinga's group); all three groups were victims as well as perpetrators. Kenya witnessed widespread incidents of arson, looting, and inter-ethnic violence, leading to a significant loss of life and displacement of people. The security forces were deployed to quell the unrest, but their actions were also met with accusations of excessive force and human rights abuses. More than 1,000 people were killed, and more than 600,000 were displaced in the election's violent aftermath as efforts to resolve the political impasse between Kibaki and Odinga (including mediation attempts by former UN secretary-general Kofi Annan) were not immediately successful.

After weeks of negotiations, the signing of the National Accord on February 28, 2008, led to the formation of a power-sharing government. President Kibaki remained in office, while Raila Odinga became the Prime Minister, with a mandate to address the underlying issues and implement necessary reforms.

The violence and political crisis that emerged from the December 2007 election highlighted deep-seated political and ethnic divisions in Kenya. It exposed shortcomings in the electoral process, the need for institutional reforms, and the importance of addressing historical grievances and power-sharing arrangements. The event served as a catalyst for subsequent constitutional reforms and efforts to strengthen democratic institutions, including the establishment of a new constitution in 2010.

In conclusion, the December 2007 election in Kenya remains a critical chapter in Kenya's political evolution. It serves as a reminder of the importance of credible and transparent elections in ensuring peace and stability.

6.4 THE 2013 ELECTION

Despite fears of violence, voting on March 4, 2013, was generally peaceful and lauded as free and transparent. Anxiety grew, however, as the announcement of final results was delayed by technical problems in the vote-tallying process. The 2013 presidential election in Kenya marked a significant turning point for the country, following the violence and turmoil that had accompanied the previous election in 2007. The election saw the triumph of Uhuru Kenyatta, who won with a decisive majority of the votes cast.

The 2013 election was notable for its peacefulness and lack of violence, in contrast to the previous one. This was largely due to the reforms that had been implemented in the intervening years, aimed at improving the electoral process and addressing the underlying causes of the violence.

One of the key reforms was the creation of the Independent Electoral and Boundaries Commission (IEBC), which was tasked with overseeing the election and ensuring it was free and fair. The IEBC worked closely with civil society groups and international observers to ensure the election was transparent and credible.

Another important development was the adoption of a new constitution in 2010, which devolved power from the central government to local authorities and improved protections for human rights. The new constitution was seen as a significant step towards addressing the underlying causes of the violence that had marred the 2007 election.

The election of Kenyatta marked a new chapter in Kenyan politics, with a renewed focus on economic growth and development. Kenyatta pursued policies to improve infrastructure, create jobs, and attract foreign investment, and oversaw a period of sustained economic growth during his first term in office.

Kenyatta inherited security issues that continued to be of concern for his administration. Kenyan troops had entered neighbouring Somalia to join in the fight against the Islamic militant group al-Shabaab in 2011. The group promised to retaliate and periodically initiated attacks on Kenyan soil. One of the largest attacks occurred in September 2013, when al-Shabaab gunmen besieged an upscale shopping mall in Nairobi, leaving more than 70 people dead and raising questions about the effectiveness of Kenya's security forces. Lower-level attacks by the group continued. Incidents in northern Kenya in late 2014, in which al-Shabaab killed dozens of non-Muslims, renewed concerns over security and led to Kenyatta appointing new officials to high-level positions in December 2014.

On April 2, 2015, al-Shabaab struck with its deadliest attack to date on Kenyan soil, when the group raided a university in Garissa early in the morning. The militants killed more than 140 people, injured more than 70, and held numerous hostages before the siege was ended later in the day.

6.5 THE 2017 ELECTIONS, ANNULMENT OF PRESIDENTIAL ELECTION

The 2017 presidential election in Kenya was another highly contested and controversial event in the country's history. Incumbent President Uhuru Kenyatta, seeking re-election, faced off against his main rival, Raila Odinga, leader of the National Super Alliance (NASA) coalition.

The election was marked by allegations of irregularities and fraud, with Odinga and his supporters claiming that the election had been rigged in favour of Kenyatta. There were also concerns about the role of technology in the electoral process, with the electronic voting system experiencing glitches and malfunctions.

Following the announcement of the results, which showed Kenyatta as the winner with 54% of the vote, Odinga and NASA rejected the results and launched legal challenges. The Supreme Court of Kenya ultimately annulled the election results, citing irregularities and illegalities, and ordered a new election to be held within 60 days.

The repeat election in October 2017 was also marked by controversy and violence. Kenyatta won the repeat election with 98% of the vote, but the low turnout and opposition boycott cast a shadow over the election's legitimacy.

Despite these challenges, the 2017 election also demonstrated the resilience and commitment of the Kenyan people to the democratic process. Civil society organizations and independent media were crucial in monitoring the election and promoting transparency and accountability. The peaceful resolution of the election dispute through legal means was also a positive development and demonstrated the strength of Kenya's judiciary.

6.6 THE 2022 ELECTION

In the presidential race, there were four candidates, Odinga and Ruto being the front-runners. Kenyatta, who was not eligible to serve another term as president, had officially endorsed Odinga in February; that same month Kenyatta also declared Ruto unfit to be president.

1. Voting was generally peaceful on August 9, and early, incomplete results showed Odinga and Ruto in a close race. Vote tallying concluded, and on August 15, IEBC head Wafula Chebukati announced that Ruto had won with 50.49% of the vote, narrowly edging past and avoiding a runoff with Odinga, who reportedly received 48.85% . However, the announcement was overshadowed by uncertainty, for earlier that day four of the seven IEBC commissioners stated that they could not support the final results due to the "opaque nature" of the last phase of the vote-tabulation process; furthermore, just prior to that, one of Odinga's election agents claimed to have reports of electoral interference, though he did not provide details. Odinga refused to recognize the results, vowed to challenge them through legal channels, and filed a challenge with the

Supreme Court later that month. His was one of nine petitions filed at the court: two were dismissed, and the remaining seven were consolidated due to their similarities.

President William Ruto

President William Ruto

President William Ruto took office on September 13, 2022. The current country's economy is burdened with debt, inflation, joblessness, and a sense of pessimism. The International Monetary Fund (IMF) has urged Kenya to broaden its tax base and eliminate fuel subsidies, adding to Ruto's challenges. Broadening the tax base means including more informal workers, known as "hustlers," in the tax net, which may upset Ruto's political supporters. Removing fuel subsidies will increase prices and further inflation, contradicting Ruto's campaign promises. However, recent fuel price hikes indicate Ruto's determination to eliminate subsidies.

During his campaign, Ruto focused on the economy and promised a radical transformation if elected. However, implementing his manifesto requires funding, new economic structures, and may face resistance from those defending the status quo. It's important to recognize that most economic policy actions take time to produce noticeable effects, which can be a political challenge when elections are based on high expectations and promises.

To revitalize the economy, Ruto should prioritize the following areas: agriculture, micro, small, and medium enterprises (MSMEs), housing and settlement, healthcare, and the digital superhighway and creative economy. Improving agricultural productivity and efficiency, supporting MSMEs with proper funding mechanisms, addressing the housing shortage, ensuring affordable healthcare through a well-managed insurance system, and promoting the digital and creative sectors are key strategies for economic revitalization.

Ruto must balance the interests of different stakeholders and communicate the time lag inherent in economic policy actions to the public effectively. Voters often expect instant results, and politicians should address this expectation while explaining the realities of economic transformation.

President Ruto faces numerous economic challenges, but by focusing on key areas and implementing targeted strategies, he can work towards revitalizing Kenya's economy. His success will be closely observed, and his approach to economics will be compared to that of previous presidents.

CHAPTER 7
MODERN KENYA

KENYA IS a country in East Africa famed for its scenic landscapes and vast wildlife preserves. At 580,367 square kilometres, Kenya is the world's 48th largest country by area. With a population of more than 47.6 million in the 2019 census, Kenya is the 27th most populous country in the world. Kenya's capital and largest city is Nairobi, while its oldest, currently second largest city, and first capital is the coastal city of Mombasa. Kisumu City is the third-largest city and an inland port on Lake Victoria. Other important urban centres include Nakuru and Eldoret. As of 2020, Kenya is the third-largest economy in sub-Saharan Africa after Nigeria and South Africa. Kenya is bordered by South Sudan to the northwest, Ethiopia to the north, Somalia to the east, Uganda to the west, Tanzania to the south, and the Indian Ocean to the southeast. Its geography, climate and population vary widely, ranging from cold snow-capped mountaintops with vast surrounding forests, wildlife, and fertile agricultural regions to temperate climate, rift valley counties, dry, less fertile arid and semi-arid areas, and absolute deserts.

Nairobi Kenya Source: www.getyourguide.com

The capital of Kenya is Nairobi, a sprawling city that, like many other African metropolises, is a study in contrasts, with modern skyscrapers looking out over vast shantytowns in the distance, many harbouring refugees fleeing civil wars in neighbouring countries. Its Indian Ocean coast provided historically important ports by which goods from Arabian and Asian traders have entered the continent for many centuries. Along that coast, which holds some of the finest beaches in Africa, are predominantly Muslim Swahili cities.

One of these cities is Mombasa, a historic centre that has contributed much to the musical and culinary heritage of the country. Inland are populous highlands famed for both their tea plantations, an economic staple during the British colonial era, and their variety of animal species, including lions, elephants, cheetahs, rhinoceroses, and hippopotamuses. Kenya's western provinces, marked by lakes and rivers, are forested, while a small portion of the north is desert and semidesert. The country's diverse wildlife and panoramic geography draw large numbers of European and North American visitors, and tourism is an important contributor to Kenya's economy.

8 Top Animals in Kenya www.kenyageographic.com

Kenya's many peoples are well known to outsiders, largely because of the British colonial administration's openness to study. Anthropologists and other social scientists have documented for generations the lives of the Maasai, Luhya, Luo, Kalenjin, and Kikuyu peoples, to name only some of the groups. Adding to the country's ethnic diversity are European and Asian immigrants from many nations. Kenyans proudly embrace their individual cultures and traditions, yet they are also cognizant of the importance of national solidarity; a motto of "Harambee" (Swahili: "Pulling together") has been stressed by Kenya's government since independence.

7.1 THE ECONOMY OF KENYA

Since independence in 1963, Kenya's economy has contained both privately owned and state-run enterprises. Most of the country's business is in private hands (with a large amount of foreign investment), but the government also shapes the country's economic development through various regulatory powers and "parastatals," or enterprises that it partly or wholly owns. This policy aims to achieve economic growth and stability, generate employment, and maximize foreign earnings by achieving high levels of agricultural exports while substituting domestically produced goods for those that have been imported. For a decade after independence, this policy showed great promise as rising wages, employment, and government revenue provided the means for expanding health services, education, transportation, and communication.

Agriculture is the largest sector of the Kenyan economy, employing over 70% of the country's population and accounting for approximately one-third of GDP. The main crops grown in Kenya include tea, coffee, horticulture products, and sugarcane, with the country being a major exporter of these products to international markets.

Manufacturing is also an important sector of the Kenyan economy, accounting for approximately 10% of GDP. The country has a diverse manufacturing base, producing a range of products, including textiles, cement, chemicals, and processed foods. The government has recently promoted industrialization and value addition, focusing on developing the country's manufacturing capacity and creating employment opportunities for young people.

The services sector is another key component of the Kenyan economy, accounting for approximately half of the GDP. The country has a vibrant tourism industry, with millions of visitors coming each year to experience Kenya's natural beauty and cultural heritage. Other important services include financial services, telecommunications, and transportation.

But problems that arose with the global oil price increase in 1973 have been aggravated by periodic droughts and accelerating population growth. Kenya's economy has been unable to maintain a favourable balance of trade while addressing the problems of chronic poverty and growing unemployment. The country's ability to industrialize has been hampered by, among other factors, limited domestic purchasing power, shrinking government budgets, increased external and internal debt, poor infrastructure, and massive governmental corruption and mismanagement.

Kenya attempted to diversify its exports in the last decade of the 20th century to decrease its dependence on volatile agricultural markets, adding horticultural products, clothing, cement, soda ash, and fluorspar. The country also prioritised exporting manufactured goods such as paper and vehicles. However, domestic import restrictions have been removed slowly, and this policy has been only partially successful. Kenya's economy, which did not grow at a constant rate during the last two decades of the 20th century, continued to be dominated by the external market; tourism and agricultural exports were still the major sources of foreign exchange for the country in the early 21st century.

The recently concluded general elections have set the stage for Kenya's next development chapter. The country has made significant political and economic reforms that have contributed to sustained economic growth, social development, and political stability gains over the past decade. Kenya's economy achieved broad-based growth averaging 4.8% per year between 2015-2019, significantly reducing poverty (from 36.5% in 2005 to 27.2% in 2019 ($2.15/day poverty line).

In 2020, the COVID-19 pandemic hit the economy hard, disrupting international trade and transport, tourism, and urban services activities. Fortunately, the agricultural sector, a cornerstone of the economy, remained resilient, helping to limit the contraction of the GDP to only 0.3%. In 2021, the economy staged a strong recovery, with the economy growing at 7.5%, although some sectors, such as tourism, remained under pressure. GDP growth is projected at 5.5% in 2022, and the poverty rate has resumed its trending decline after rising earlier in the pandemic.

Kenya's economy continued to rebound from the pandemic in 2022, with the real gross domestic product (GDP) increasing by 6% year-on-year in the first half of 2022, driven by broad-based increases in services and industry. Global commodity price shocks dampened this recovery, as did the long regional drought and uncertainty during the 2022 general elections.

A recent rapid response phone survey that monitors the impact of shocks on households shows a rise in food insecurity, most severely in rural areas, where over half of the households reduced their food consumption in June 2022. Most households reported increased prices of essential food items, with many unable to access core staples, such as beans or maize. In response to the inflationary pressures, the Central Bank of Kenya (CBK) has raised the policy rate thrice since May 2022 by a cumulative 175 basis points to reach 8.75%.

Boosting food resilience through community interventions in arid and semi-arid lands and supporting farmer groups to join sustainable value chains will help feed Kenya during drought periods better.

Kenya's medium-term growth prospects remain positive, with the GDP projected to grow by 5.2% on average in 2023–24, notwithstanding current global and domestic shocks. The baseline assumes robust growth of credit to the private sector, continued low COVID-19 infection rates, a near-term recovery in agricultural production, and high commodity prices favourable to Kenyan exports. These developments are in turn expected to catalyse private investment to support economic growth over the medium term.

7.2 KENYA'S EXPORTS

Kenya exported an estimated $7.4 billion worth of products around the globe in 2022. That dollar reflects a 22.2% upturn over the last five years, starting with $6.05 billion in 2018.

Based on the average exchange rate for 2022, the Kenyan shilling depreciated by -16.4% against the US dollar since 2018 and fell by -7.5% from 2021 to 2022. Kenya's weaker local currency makes its exports paid for in stronger US dollars relatively less expensive for international buyers. Year over year, Kenya's export revenues increased by 12% from $6 billion in 2020.

The top 5 most valuable products exported from Kenya are tea, fresh or dried flowers, processed petroleum oils, coffee, titanium ores, and concentrates.

Kenya's Largest Trading Partners

The latest available country-specific data shows that over two-thirds (68%) of products exported from Kenya were bought by importers in Uganda (11.1% of the Kenyan total), United States of America (9.2%), the Netherlands (8%), Pakistan (7.4%), Tanzania (6.6%), United Kingdom (5.12%), United Arab Emirates (5.06%), Rwanda (4.6%), mainland China (3.2%), Egypt (3.1%), South Sudan (2.7%), and the Democratic Republic of the Congo (2%).

From a continental perspective, 41% of Kenya's exports by value were delivered to fellow African countries. Kenya also sold 26.2% to importers in Asia. Kenya shipped another 22.5% worth of goods to Europe. Smaller percentages went to buyers in North America (9.7%), Oceania (0.4%) led by Australia, then Latin America (0.2%), excluding Mexico but including the Caribbean.

By harnessing the potential of trade within the continent, Kenya can unlock economic growth, diversify its markets, create jobs, foster regional integration, facilitate knowledge transfer, and promote cultural exchange. These advantages contribute to Kenya's development agenda and support the broader vision of an integrated and prosperous Africa.

Given Kenya's population of 50.9 million people, it is a total of $7.4 billion in 2022 exported goods, translating to roughly $145 for every resident in the East African country. That dollar metric is a flatlining gain from the average of $140 per person one year earlier in 2021.

Advantages of Intra-African Trade over Other International Trade

Intra-African trade offers

Kenya's large volume of Intra-Africa trading presents several advantages compared to international trade outside the African continent.

Reduced dependency on External Markets: Intra-African trade allows countries to reduce their reliance on external markets and diversify their trade relationships. Depending solely on international trade partners outside the continent makes countries vulnerable to global economic fluctuations, geopolitical tensions, and protectionist measures. By fostering intra-African trade, countries can create a more balanced and resilient trade portfolio, mitigating risks associated with overdependence on a limited number of trading partners.

Proximity and Lower Transportation Costs: One significant advantage of intra-African trade is the geographical proximity of countries within the continent. Compared to long-distance international trade, neighbouring African nations can access markets more easily and at a lower cost. Reduced transportation costs and shorter transit times increase trade logistics efficiency, making it more economically viable for businesses to engage in cross-border transactions. This advantage promotes competitiveness and facilitates the growth of regional value chains.

Cultural and Linguistic Affinities: African countries share common cultural, historical, and linguistic affinities that can foster greater cooperation and understanding in trade. Shared cultural elements and similar business practices facilitate communication, negotiation, and trust-building among trading partners. These commonalities can lead to smoother trade transactions, better business relationships, and more effective collaboration in various sectors.

Market Expansion and Business Opportunities: Intra-African trade provides a vast market for African businesses to explore and expand their customer base. The African continent is home to over 1.3 billion people, representing a significant consumer market with diverse needs and preferences. By tapping into this market, businesses can identify new opportunities, increase sales, and drive revenue growth. Moreover, expanding intra-African trade opens avenues for entrepreneurial ventures and supports the development of small and medium-sized enterprises (SMEs), which are crucial drivers of job creation and economic development.

Regional Integration and Infrastructure Development: Intra-African trade plays a pivotal role in promoting regional integration and the development of essential infrastructure. Trade agreements and regional economic communities, such as the African Continental Free Trade Area (AfCFTA) and the East African Community (EAC), facilitate the removal of trade barriers, harmonize regulations, and improve cross-border infrastructure. These efforts boost connectivity, enhance transport networks, and reduce trade costs, making it easier for goods and services to flow across borders. Improved infrastructure benefits not only intra-African trade but also international trade, as it strengthens a country's overall trade capacity.

Development of Pan-African Industries and Value Chains: Intra-African trade fosters the development of pan-African industries and value chains. Collaboration among African countries in sectors such as manufacturing, agriculture, and services leads to the specialization of production and the integration of supply chains. This process enhances productivity, improves competitiveness, and creates opportunities for economies of scale. The growth of pan-African industries strengthens the continent's position in global markets and contributes to the overall economic development of African nations.

In summary, intra-African trade offers advantages such as reduced dependency on external markets, proximity and lower transportation costs, cultural and linguistic affinities, market expansion, regional integration, and the development of pan-African industries. These benefits contribute to the growth, diversification, and resilience of African economies, creating business opportunities and fostering greater cooperation among African nations.

7.3 KENYA'S TOP 10 EXPORTS

The following export product groups represent the highest dollar value in Kenyan global shipments during 2022. Also shown is the percentage share each export category represents in terms of overall exports from Kenya.

- Coffee, tea, and spices: $1.7 billion (23.4% of total exports)
- Live trees, plants, and cut flowers: $694.2 million (9.4%)
- Mineral fuels, including oil: $450.8 million (6.1%)
- Ores, slag, ash: $335.9 million (4.5%)
- Animal/vegetable fats, oils, waxes: $310.5 million (4.2%)
- Fruits, nuts: $279.3 million (3.8%)

- Clothing, accessories (not knit or crochet): $225.4 million (3%)
- Vegetables: $215.5 million (2.9%)
- Iron, steel: $201.7 million (2.7%)
- Knit or crochet clothing and accessories: $174.3 million (2.4%)

By value, Kenya's top 10 exports generated over three-fifths (62.5%) of the overall value of its global shipments. Mineral fuels, including oil, represent the fastest grower among the top 10 export categories, up by 61.3% from 2021 to 2022. The second place for improving export sales was animal or vegetable fats, oils and waxes, with a 43.2% advance.

Kenya's shipments of the ores, slag and ash product category posted the third-fastest gain in value, up by 29.9%. Kenyan international sales of titanium ores and concentrates were a strong driver for that increase. There was a pair of double-digit declines : Kenya's exports of vegetables (down -28.7% from 2021) and live trees, plants, and cut flowers (down -13.8%).

At the more granular four-digit Harmonized Tariff System code level, tea, including flavoured varieties, represents Kenya's most valuable exported product at 18.7% of the African country's total. In second place were fresh or dried flowers for bouquets or orna-mental purposes (8.5%) trailed by refined petroleum oils (5.7%), coffee (4.4%), titanium ores and concentrates (3.4%), palm oil (2.6%), dates, figs, pineapples, mangoes, avocadoes and guavas (2.3%), plated or coated items made from flat-rolled iron or non-alloy steel (1.9%), medication mixes in dosage (also 1.9%), and, finally, unknitted and non-crocheted men's suits or trousers (1.5%).

7.4 PRODUCTS DRIVING KENYA'S LARGEST TRADING SURPLUSES

The following types of Kenyan product shipments represent positive net exports or a trade balance surplus. Investopedia defines net exports as the value of a country's total exports minus the value of its total imports. In a nutshell, net exports represent the amount by which foreign spending on a home country's goods or services exceeds the home country's spending on foreign goods or services.

1. Coffee, tea, spices: $1.7 billion (Up by 19.4% since 2021)
2. Live trees, plants, cut flowers: $684 million (Down by -14%)
3. Ores, slag, ash: $304 million (Up by 23.9%)
4. Fruits, nuts: $246.6 million (Up by 0.1%)
5. Vegetables: $150.6 million (Down by -42.1%)
6. Clothing, accessories (not knit or crochet): $129.3 million (Up by 9.8%)
7. Knit or crochet clothing, and accessories: $117.9 million (Down by -1.1%)
8. Meat: $88 million (Up by 26.8%)
9. Salt, sulphur, stone, cement: $84.6 million (Up by 40.8%)
10. Tobacco, manufactured substitutes: $81.3 million (Down by -14.7%)

Kenya has highly positive net exports in international trade principally for tea, coffee, and spices like ginger, pepper, cloves, and vanilla.

7.5 PRODUCTS BEHIND KENYA'S WORST TRADING DEFICITS

Kenya incurred an estimated -$13.7 billion trade deficit for 2022, up by 9.5% from -$12.5 billion in red ink one year earlier in 2021. Below are exports from Kenya that resulted in negative net exports or product trade balance deficits. These negative net exports reveal product categories in which foreign spending on Kenya's goods trail Kenyan importer spending on foreign products.

1. Mineral fuels, including oil: -$5.14 billion (Up by 59.9% since 2021)
2. Machinery including computers: -$1.34 billion (Down by -8.5%)
3. Cereals: -$1.2 billion (Up by 19.3%)
4. Iron, steel: -$1.04 billion (Down by -7.5%)
5. Electrical machinery, equipment: -$1 billion (Down by -9.7%)
6. Vehicles: -$967.7 million (Down by -26%)
7. Animal/vegetable fats, oils, waxes: -$845.4 million (Up by 0.7%)
8. Plastics, plastic articles: -$821.2 million (Down by -2.5%)
9. Pharmaceuticals: -$609.8 million (Down by -4.6%)
10. Paper, paper items: -$403.8 million (Up by 14.1%)

Therefore, Kenya has highly negative net exports and deep international trade deficits for mineral fuels, particularly refined petroleum oils, petroleum gases, and coal.

7.6 KENYAN EXPORT COMPANIES

According to MarcoPolis.net rankings, the following are the top 10 Kenyan companies. Six of these companies are banks, which can support Kenya's international trade projects.

- Safaricom (telecommunications)
- East African Breweries (beverages)
- Equity Banking (banking)
- Kenya Commercial Bank (banking)
- British American Tobacco (tobacco)
- Standard Chartered Bank (banking)
- Co-operative Bank of Kenya (banking)

- Lafarge-Bamburi Cement (cement)
- Barclays Bank (banking)
- Diamond Trust Bank (banking)

7.7 AGRICULTURE, FORESTRY, AND FISHING

Agriculture plays an important role in Kenya's economy. Although its share of gross domestic product (GDP) has declined —from more than two-fifths in 1964 to less than one-fifth in the early 21st century—agriculture supplies the manufacturing sector with raw materials. It generates tax revenue and foreign exchange that support the rest of the economy. Moreover, it employs the majority of the population.

In the first years after independence, the government sought to redistribute the land on which most of the agricultural exports were produced. Although there are now thousands of large farms, ranches, and plantations, the majority of the farms are smaller than five acres (two hectares). Tea and fresh flowers are the key foreign-exchange earners; Sisal, cotton, and fruits and vegetables also are important cash crops. Historically, coffee has been an important foreign exchange earner, and it is still contributing to the economy, but it began declining in importance and earnings in the 1990s, partly due to market instability and deregulation.

Kenya supplies most of the pyrethrum (a flower used to create the non-synthetic pesticide pyrethrin) to the world market; demand for this product fluctuates depending upon the level of interest in the United States, which is the largest consumer of this commodity. National boards controlling key export crops such as coffee, tea, and cotton were deregulated in the early 1990s.

The major crops for domestic consumption are corn (maize) and wheat. Sugarcane was an export crop in the 1970s and '80s, but by the '90s, domestic demand exceeded the supply and had to be imported. Livestock (including cattle and goats) is raised, dairy goods are produced primarily for domestic use, and the government maintains a reserve supply of such commodities as skim milk powder, cheese, and butter. Surplus animal and dairy products are exported.

Despite the importance of agriculture to the country's economic well-being, the lack of water, infrastructure, and arable land (less than one-tenth of Kenya can be used for agriculture) seriously constrains further expansion. Although the government has made efforts to increase irrigation, it is estimated that only one-fifth to one-fourth of the potentially irrigable area has been developed.

Forests occupy only a small portion of the land but are extremely important in the domestic economy. Most of the forest reserves are wooded bush, bamboo, and grass; the remainder consists of planted softwoods, which now support a domestic paper industry. Forests are vital for conserving Kenya's soil and water resources, but they are increasingly threatened by a fast-growing population that constantly demands more fuel and settlement areas. As fuel, wood is used primarily for domestic cooking, but deforestation threatens the supply. A tree-planting program has been initiated to grow quick-maturing indigenous and exotic species in ecologically suitable areas.

Fish and marine products represent a small but growing portion of Kenya's economy and are locally important. Freshwater fish from Lakes Victoria and Rudolf constitute the bulk of the catch. The encroaching water hyacinth on the surface of Lake Victoria threatened this fishery in the 1990s, although several strategies, including the introduction of weevils into the environment, countered this nuisance. Most of the weed has been successfully eliminated, although the potential for a resurgence remains.

7.8 THE DIVERSE LANDSCAPE OF KENYA

Kenya's geography and natural resources have significantly shaped the country's history, culture, and economy. Kenya's geography is characterized by several distinct regions, each with its unique features and resources. Kenya's landscape is incredibly diverse, with various terrains and environments that have significantly shaped the country's history, culture, and economy. The following sections provide an overview of the different regions that make up Kenya's diverse landscape.

Coastal Region

Kenya's coastal region is situated along the Indian Ocean and is characterised by long sandy beaches, coral reefs, and mangrove forests. The region's climate is hot and humid, with temperatures averaging around 30°C (86°F) year-round. The coastal region is home to several historic towns and ports, such as Mombasa and Lamu, which have played a crucial role in the region's trade and commerce.

Inland Plateaus and Highlands

The inland plateaus and highlands are situated in the central and western parts of the country and are characterized by rolling hills and expansive plains. The region is the site of several rivers, including the Tana and the Ewaso Nyiro, which provide water for irrigation, hydroelectric power generation, and wildlife habitats. The highlands are also home to several national parks and game reserves, such as the Aberdare Range, the Maasai Mara, and the Mount Kenya National Park.

Great Rift Valley

The Great Rift Valley runs through Kenya from north to south and is a massive geological formation that includes several lakes, volcanoes, and mountains. The valley is home to several lakes, including Lake Victoria, the largest freshwater lake in Africa, and

Lake Turkana, the largest desert lake in the world. The valley is also the site of several important national parks and wildlife reserves, such as the Hell's Gate National Park and the Lake Nakuru National Park.

Northern Region

Arid and semi-arid landscapes, including deserts, savannas, and scrublands, characterise Kenya's northern region. The region is home to several unique wildlife species, such as the Grevy's zebra and the Somali ostrich, and is an important area for pastoralism and nomadic herding.

Eastern Region

Low-lying plains characterize Kenya's eastern region, home to several important wildlife reserves, such as the Tsavo East and Tsavo West National Parks. The region is also the site of several important agricultural areas, including the Tana River Delta and the Galana-Kulalu irrigation scheme.

Kenya's diverse landscape has provided both opportunities and challenges for its development. The country's fertile soils, abundant water resources, and diverse wildlife have provided the foundation for agricultural development, tourism, and conservation. At the same time, the country's arid and semi-arid regions have presented challenges to food security and sustainable livelihoods.

The exploitation and management of Kenya's natural resources have been a subject of both conservation and exploitation. The government and civil society organizations have tried to protect and conserve Kenya's wildlife, forests, and water resources by establishing national parks, forest reserves, and conservation programs. At the same time, the government has sought to exploit the country's mineral and energy resources to boost economic growth and development.

Kenya's diverse landscape also presents challenges to infrastructure development and connectivity. The country's rugged terrain and expansive size have made providing infrastructure and connecting communities challenging. However, the government has significantly invested in infrastructure development, including road and railway networks, to improve connectivity and boost economic development.

In conclusion, Kenya's diverse landscape provides the foundation for its economic, social, and cultural development. Understanding the different regions and their unique features and challenges is essential to appreciating the country's potential and obstacles for sustainable development. The exploitation and management of Kenya's natural resources require careful consideration and planning to ensure that they benefit all Kenyans and contribute to sustainable development.

7.9 MINERAL RESOURCES

Kenya is endowed with mineral resources such as limestone, soda ash, salt, fluorspar, titanium, gold, coal, and oil. Soda ash (used in glassmaking) is Kenya's most valuable mineral export and is quarried at Lake Magadi in the Rift Valley. Limestone deposits at the coast and the interior are exploited for cement manufacture and agriculture. Vermiculite, gold, rubies, topazes, and salt are also important, as is fluorite (also known as fluorspar and used in metallurgy), which is mined along the Kerio River in the north. Titanium- and zirconium-bearing sand deposits were found in multiple locations northeast of Mombasa and to the south of the city. Exploration for petroleum has so far met with limited success. The country has been prospecting and mining minerals for many years, with significant discoveries made recently. For example, the discovery of oil in Turkana County in 2012 could transform Kenya's economy and boost its energy security.

In conclusion, Kenya's abundant mineral resources are a critical contributor to its economy and development. The exploitation and management of these resources require careful planning and consideration to ensure that they benefit all Kenyans and contribute to sustainable development.

7.10 NATURAL RESOURCES

Kenya's natural resources are diverse, ranging from minerals to wildlife, forests, and water resources.

Arable Land - Kenya has significant arable land, with an estimated 10% of its total land area suitable for agriculture. The country's agricultural sector is vital to its economy, employing over 70% of the population and contributing to over 30% of its GDP. The country's fertile soils, favourable climate, and abundant water resources provide a conducive environment for producing crops such as tea, coffee, maize, and horticultural products. The potential for economic development through agriculture can be realised by improving productivity and value addition. The government and private sector have made efforts to promote commercial farming, irrigation, and value addition in the agricultural sector.

Wildlife - Kenya is renowned for its abundant wildlife, with over 50 national parks and game reserves such as the Maasai Mara, Amboseli, and Tsavo National Parks providing habitat for diverse wildlife species and important ecosystem services such as pollination and pest control. Wildlife tourism contributes to the country's economy, generating over $1 billion in revenue annually. The country is home to a wide range of wildlife, including the Big Five (elephant, lion, leopard, buffalo, and rhinoceros) and numerous bird species and reptiles.

The annual wildebeest migration is best observed at the Maasai Mara National Reserve, including a Maasai village. Amboseli National Park, a former home of the Maasai, lies at the foot of

Mount Kilimanjaro. Marsabit National Park and Reserve in the north is noted for its populations of large mammals such as lions, elephants, rhinoceroses, zebras, and giraffes. Tsavo East and Tsavo West National Parks are noted for their abundant wildlife and diverse landscapes. Mzima Springs, found in Tsavo West, have clear pools of fresh water that provide ideal conditions for viewing hippopotamuses, crocodiles, and fish. Sibiloi National Park, in the far northern part of the country, contains sites where scientists from the University of Nairobi (including Richard Leakey) have excavated hominid, remains since 1968. Mount Kenya National Park was designated a UNESCO World Heritage site in 1997.

The Lake Turkana National Parks, comprising three national parks in the Eastern province, were named World Heritage sites beginning in 1997. Lamu Old Town, in Coast province, contains beautiful examples of Swahili architecture; it became a World Heritage site in 2001. In 2008 the Sacred Mijikenda Kaya Forests—several forests containing the remains of villages (kaya) once inhabited by the Mijikenda (Nyika) people and now considered sacred—were collectively designated a World Heritage site.

National Archives - The Kenya National Archives and Documentation Service in Nairobi, housed in a building that was originally the Bank of India, holds an increasing number of government and historical documents and exhibits of arts and crafts and photographs. A national library service board has been established to equip, maintain, and develop libraries in Kenya, including a branch library service. The McMillan Memorial Library in Nairobi has books, newspapers, and a parliamentary archive. The National Museum, also in Nairobi, contains archaeological remains and objects of traditional material culture.

Forests - Kenya has several forests and forest reserves, including the Aberdare Range, the Mau Forest Complex, and the Mount Kenya Forest Reserve, covering about 6% of the country's total land area. The forests are a source of timber, fuelwood, and other forest products, as well as wildlife habitat and provide important ecosystem services such as water collection and climate regulation. Forests also play a critical role in Kenya's economy and ecology. The forests provide vital habitats for wildlife, regulate water cycles, and provide resources for local communities.

Water Resources - Kenya's water resources, with several rivers, lakes, and underground aquifers, are critical to the country's economy and livelihoods. The country has several rivers, lakes, and aquifers, which are used for irrigation, hydroelectric power generation, and domestic and industrial use. However, pollution, over-extraction, and climate change threaten the country's water resources.

Kenya's economic development has been tied to its ability to improve energy resources. The emphasis since independence has been on producing hydroelectricity, but access to energy is limited in rural areas since the bulk of electricity is consumed by the two major urban centres of Nairobi and Mombasa. There are hydro-electric plants located on the Tana and Turkwel rivers. Geothermal resources in the Rift Valley have been tapped since the early 1980s to generate electricity and have come to supply a significant amount of Nairobi's total needs. While the expansion of generating capacity continued through grants, a severe drought occurred in the northwest part of the country at the end of the 20th century. This led to blackouts that continued into the beginning of the 21st century.

Kenya's natural resources have also been the subject of conservation and exploitation. The country's wildlife, forests, and water resources have come under increasing pressure from human activities, including poaching, deforestation, and water pollution. The government and civil society organizations have tried to protect and conserve these resources by establishing national parks, forest reserves, and conservation programs. At the same time, the government has sought to exploit the country's mineral and energy resources to boost economic growth and development.

The relationship between Kenya's geography, natural resources, and development is complex and multifaceted. The country's diverse terrain and resources provide both opportunities and challenges for sustainable development. For example, the country's fertile soils and abundant water resources provide the potential for agricultural development but also require careful management to avoid environmental degradation and water scarcity. Similarly, the country's mineral resources have the potential to generate wealth and create employment opportunities but must be managed in a way that benefits local communities and promotes sustainable development. For example:

Resource exploitation can lead to economic development in a country when properly managed. Given the country's abundant natural resources, the potential for economic development through resource exploitation in Kenya is significant.

However, resource exploitation can also negatively impact local communities' environment, health, and social well-being. Proper management and regulation of resource exploitation are essential to mitigate these negative impacts and ensure that the benefits of resource exploitation are shared equitably.

One challenge that Kenya faces in realizing the potential for economic development through resource exploitation is corruption. Corruption undermines effective governance, reduces investor confidence, and perpetuates poverty. To address this challenge, the government must strengthen institutions, promote transparency and accountability, and promote public participation in decision-making processes.

In conclusion, Kenya's potential for economic development through resource exploitation is significant. The country's abundant natural resources provide a foundation for economic growth and development. However, exploiting and managing these resources must be balanced with conservation efforts and the well-being of local communities. The government, private sector, and civil society organizations have a crucial role to play in ensuring that resource exploitation contributes to sustainable economic development in Kenya. Addressing corruption, promoting environmental sustainability, and ensuring the rights of local communities must be at the forefront of these efforts.

CHAPTER 8
KENYA'S INDUSTRY AND INFRASTRUCTURE

8.1 MANUFACTURING

KENYA IS the most industrially developed country in East Africa, yet it has not yet produced results to match its potential. Manufacturing is based largely on processing imported goods, although the government supports the development of export-oriented industries. Major industries include agricultural processing, publishing and printing, and the manufacture of textiles and clothing, cement, tires, batteries, paper, ceramics, and leather goods. Assembly plants, which utilize imported parts, produce various kinds of commercial and passenger vehicles and even export a small quantity to other African countries such as Uganda, Tanzania, Rwanda, and Burundi.

Steel processing for reexport and the construction industry is growing, with about a dozen steel mills in operation. The petroleum industry, which was deregulated in 1994, produces diesel and jet fuel from imported crude oil at a refinery near Mombasa and provides a major source of foreign exchange.

Agricultural products such as tea, fresh flowers, fruits and vegetables, and coffee constitute the greatest proportion of Kenya's exports. The remainder of the exports consists of petroleum products, cement, hides and skins, and soda ash. Imports include machinery, transport equipment, chemical, petroleum, and food and beverages. Among Kenya's chief trading partners are India, China, Uganda, and Pakistan. Kenya is a member of the East African Community Customs Union.

8.2 SERVICES

Kenya is home to some of the world's rarest and most interesting wildlife species. Because of this, tourism is one of the country's major sources of foreign exchange, with visitors coming largely from countries of the European Union. Tourism revolves around a basic framework of national parks, game reserves, and game sanctuaries, where various animals and cultural attractions can be enjoyed. The number of tourists began to vary annually in the early 1990s following a period of political unrest and attacks on tourists; it declined again in the early 2000s, owing partially to the threat of terrorism.

8.3 TRANSPORTATION AND TELECOMMUNICATIONS

The transportation infrastructure that developed before and after independence allowed Kenya to emerge as a viable state. Roads became the primary link between the urban areas and the rural hinterlands, although they were developed in colonial times as a subsidiary of the railway line running from Mombasa to the western parts of the country. After independence, the heavily utilized trunk and primary roads were upgraded from dirt to bitumen and gravel. As this network was expanded, freight traffic within Kenya, Tanzania, Uganda, Sudan (including what is now South Sudan), and Ethiopia increased rapidly. The heavy traffic severely damaged Kenyan roads, requiring expensive repairs.

Railways, the second most important mode of transport after roads, are operated by Kenya Railways. The main line runs northwest from Mombasa through Nairobi, Nakuru, and Eldoret to the Ugandan border. Major branch lines run from Nakuru to Kisumu on Lake Victoria and from Nairobi to Nanyuki near Mount Kenya; another goes into Tanzania. Privatization of Kenya Railways began early in the 21st century, and efforts were undertaken to make the railways more competitive in the freight market. Passenger service constitutes a very small share of the railway business.

The strategic location of Kenya on the western shores of the Indian Ocean, with easy connections to different parts of Africa, the Middle East, and Asia, has greatly enhanced the role of the international airports at Nairobi and Mombasa. Another international airport is located at Eldoret. There are domestic airports at Kisumu and Malindi and many smaller airfields throughout the country. Kenya Airways, established in 1977, privatized its operations and financial control in 1996.

Mombasa, the country's principal port, handles the bulk of the import and export traffic not only of Kenya but of Burundi, Rwanda, Uganda, and the eastern part of the Democratic Republic of the Congo. The ports of Lamu and Malindi serve mainly the coastal trade and fisheries.

Telephone service has greatly expanded since the early 1980s. However, while the number of telephones more than doubled between 1984 and 1995, most of the population still could not access local telephone lines. Cellular telephone service experienced rapid growth around the turn of the century, as did Internet access—by the mid-2000s, the country had one of the highest Internet users in sub-Saharan Africa. Like other industries in Kenya, telecommunications were privatized at the start of the 21st century.

8.4 HEALTH AND WELFARE

Together with improved housing, education, sanitation, and nutrition, healthcare programs have drastically reduced mortality rates from pre-independence levels, especially for infants. However, high rates of malaria, gastroenteritis, diarrhoea and dysentery, trachoma, amebiasis, and schistosomiasis continue, and illustrate how difficult it is to eradicate mosquitoes and provide clean water, especially in the countryside. By the beginning of the 21st century, AIDS had become the major disease in Kenya and threatened to reverse the declining death rate. Kenya, like other countries in Africa suffering under the AIDS pandemic, has utilized a number of strategies to combat the disease, including drug therapy. Some drug companies lowered their prices in Kenya by more than half in the early 21st century, but this was not enough to make drugs available to all who needed them. An inadequate supply of drugs is also a problem.

Kenyatta National Hospital in Nairobi is the country's chief referral and teaching institution, and there are also provincial and district hospitals. In rural areas, health centres and dispensaries offer diagnostic services, obstetric care, and outpatient treatment, although they often lack adequate facilities, trained personnel, and medications.

8.5 HOUSING

In rural areas, the average home consists of a two-room dwelling made with wood siding and a roof of sheet iron; for the very poor, simple grass-thatched huts are typical. The representative middle-class home in urban areas has two bedrooms, indoor plumbing, a kitchen, and a living area.

Providing housing for the urban poor has been increasingly difficult since independence. Most of the urban population lives in informal housing areas not recognized by the government, which often razes slums without warning. To provide better-quality affordable housing, new building materials are being developed. One such product is brick made from a combination of water, soil, and a small amount of cement.

8.6 EDUCATION OF KENYA

The national educational system consists of eight years of compulsory primary education (beginning at age six), four years at the secondary level, and four years of higher education. The government provides free primary and secondary education. Entrance into secondary school is contingent upon obtaining the Kenyan Certificate of Primary Education by passing a national exam.

Education for the indigenous population was not a priority of the British colonial government. After independence, however, primary and secondary school enrolment expanded markedly. Jomo Kenyatta, Kenya's first president, promised free primary education to all citizens in 1963, a promise only partially fulfilled when fees for the first four years of primary school were abolished in 1974. One consequence of this educational expansion was that underemployment and unemployment increased as better-educated citizens entered the job market. The government responded by expanding the civil service in the late 1970s, but by the early 1990s, it could no longer absorb this population. The problem was compounded as the number of secondary schools grew.

The government simultaneously pursued a policy of "education for self-reliance," whereby education was oriented toward preparing students for employment in agriculture and business. Universal free education was introduced for all years of primary schooling in 2002. In the following years, primary schools could not accommodate the increased demand for services and faced such problems as overcrowding and a lack of resources.

Education is still highly valued in Kenya, with many students pursuing "shadow education" (after-school and weekend tutoring) and remaining in a grade for more than one year to pass the Certificate of Primary Education exam. Because of the country's continuing economic problems, many of these students cannot attend school beyond the primary level; free secondary schooling was introduced in 2008 to help address this issue. Kenya's literacy rate, at more than four-fifths of the population, is high for sub-Saharan Africa.

Public universities include the University of Nairobi (1956) and Kenyatta University (1972) in Nairobi, Moi University (1984) in Eldoret, and Egerton University (1939) in Njoro, as well as the Jomo Kenyatta University of Agriculture and Technology (1981) in Nairobi. Specialized colleges include Kenya Conservatoire of Music (1944), Kenya Medical Training College (1924), and Kenya Polytechnic (1961) in Nairobi and Rift Valley Institute of Science and Technology (1972) in Nakuru.

CHAPTER 9

HOW KENYA'S TECH INDUSTRY CHANGED THE WORLD

THE U.S. HAS LONG BEEN HAILED as the global leader in financial technology innovation. However, over the past few decades, China has emerged as a formidable competitor, leveraging smartphones and social apps to pioneer remote payments and digitized money management. Nevertheless, Africa has recently emerged as a hotbed of FinTech activity, with countries like Nigeria and Kenya spearheading groundbreaking initiatives that utilize affordable and accessible technology to mobilize consumers in unprecedented ways.

9.1 KENYA'S FINTECH AND ITS EXPLOSIVE GROWTH:

FinTech refers to the application of technology and innovation to meet the financial needs of consumers and businesses. It encompasses various areas such as credit cards, online banking, and blockchain-powered cryptocurrencies. Over the past decade, FinTech has experienced explosive growth, with venture capitalists, traditional finance firms, governments, and even everyday smartphone users contributing to its development. Advancements like remote payments, app-based stock trading, and automated insurance claims have become commonplace, with the sector attracting over $50 billion in investment during the first half of the 2010s.

The Three Waves of FinTech Innovation:

The development of modern FinTech can be traced back to three distinct waves of innovation, each centred in a specific region and period. The U.S. spearheaded the first wave when it introduced transformative technologies that still shape our financial landscape today. Innovations like the Diners Club Card, introduced in the early 1950s, revolutionized payment efficiency and extended credit to consumers seamlessly. The 1960s saw the emergence of the Bankograph and the prototype of an automated teller machine (ATM), further solidifying the U.S.'s leadership in FinTech. The proliferation of the Internet in the 1990s led to the birth of online banking, further expanding banking and credit services beyond physical branches.

The second wave of FinTech, predominantly driven by Asia, began in the 2000s and continues to dominate today. China, in particular, made significant strides with smartphone apps and mobile-based financial services. The country's FinTech market reached $25.5 billion in 2018, accounting for 46% of global FinTech investments. Platforms like WeChat and Alipay have become widely adopted payment systems, enabling even rural vendors and labourers to utilize personalized QR codes for transactions. Companies such as Tencent and Alibaba have made substantial investments, disrupting traditional finance firms in areas like wealth management and credit scoring.

9.2 THE AFRICAN FINTECH WAVE:

Together with the proliferation of mobile phones, Africa become the centre of the third wave of FinTech innovation. Although the continent is still in the early stages of universal smartphone and internet use, the adoption of mobile phones has spurred economic growth. This wave is defined by inclusive mobile banking services, particularly in countries like Kenya. With mobile penetration rates surpassing the total population, Kenya has witnessed the rapid growth of FinTech innovations. Safaricom, a leading telecommunications company, introduced the M-Pesa mobile money transfer service in 2007, revolutionizing banking for the unbanked and underbanked. Through a nationwide network of over 110,000 agents, individuals can conduct transactions without needing an internet connection. Equitel, a mobile virtual network operator, has further expanded financial inclusion by offering comprehensive banking services on mobile devices. These innovations have significantly increased financial inclusion in Kenya, with 83% of the population now having access to basic financial services.

9.3 THE IMPACT OF AFRICAN FINTECH BEYOND KENYA:

Kenya's success in FinTech has become a model for other African countries. Twenty-four nations have committed to a Digital Economy Blueprint inspired by Kenya's example. The impact of these initiatives is spreading across the continent. The Global System for Mobile Communications (GSMA) reports that mobile penetration in West Africa has doubled over the past decade, with mobile payments and banking driving development in its 15 member states. In 2018 alone, the region witnessed a 23 million mobile money account surge. FinTech is important in empowering marginalized groups, such as women, the rural poor, and the displaced, by providing them with a gateway to financial empowerment.

The Importance of African FinTech for Global Innovation:

The rise of FinTech in Africa represents a significant shift in the global landscape of financial innovation. While the U.S. and China have led the way in previous waves, Africa's FinTech revolution demonstrates that innovation can occur even in regions with limited access to traditional infrastructure. By leveraging mobile technology and embracing digital solutions, African countries like Kenya are leapfrogging over traditional stages of development, paving the way for inclusive financial systems.

Moreover, the success of African FinTech serves as a wake-up call for U.S. banks and FinTech companies. They must recognize the potential of African markets and learn from the factors driving success in countries like Kenya. Embracing affordability, accessibility, and innovative business models is crucial for remaining competitive in the rapidly evolving FinTech landscape.

In conclusion, the rise of African FinTech, particularly exemplified by the success of Kenya, has reshaped the global narrative of financial innovation. Each wave of FinTech innovation has left its mark on the financial sector's evolution from the U.S. to China and Africa. Africa's FinTech wave, driven by mobile technology and inclusive services, has brought financial inclusion to millions and opened new avenues for economic growth. To stay at the forefront of global FinTech innovation, U.S. banks and FinTech companies must study and learn from the factors enabling these successes abroad. By embracing the lessons learned from African FinTech, they can adapt their strategies, products, and services to meet the evolving needs of consumers in an increasingly interconnected world

9.4 WHAT THE WORLD CAN LEARN FROM KENYA'S FINTECH'S SUCCESS STORIES

Kenya's FinTech success stories have garnered global attention and offer valuable lessons for companies worldwide. By examining these success stories, we can identify three actionable themes that can guide companies in their pursuit of innovative FinTech solutions.

Theme 1: Bundled Feature Delivery

One crucial lesson from Kenya's FinTech landscape is the power of bundled feature delivery. Equity Bank's remarkable rise from 66th to 2nd place in the market was attributed to its one-stop-shop appeal. This preference for bundled services is not exclusive to the African market; even in the United States, over 50% of product searches begin on Amazon, where 44% of online purchases occur. The trend toward universal solutions extends to FinTech and retail alike. Companies looking to emulate Kenya's success should recognize the value of offering bundled services that minimize consumer search and implementation costs.

Theme 2: Building Trust

Trust is the cornerstone of the financial industry, and Kenya's FinTech companies have effectively leveraged this aspect to their advantage. While traditional banks in the United States are aware of the importance of trust, they often struggle to translate it into cutting-edge products. In contrast, young FinTech firms possess the agility to innovate but lack the long-established trust associated with traditional institutions. Kenya's FinTech success can be attributed, in part, to the strategic combination of trusted and emerging brands. For instance, Equitel, a hybrid firm, capitalized on consumer trust in Equity Bank and Airtel, two well-established brands. U.S. companies seeking to learn from Kenya's example should explore partnerships that allow them to offer innovative services built upon trusted venues.

Theme 3: Identifying Technology Enablers

Technology enablers are often subtle yet critical conditions or infrastructures that enhance the likelihood of a technology's success. These enablers may not be recent innovations but can be repurposed from dying or outdated models. Amazon's use of intermediating warehouses, which were expected to become obsolete with the rise of direct shipping, served as an enabler for their online platform. In the context of African FinTech, Safaricom's utilization of widely spread agents to kick-start M-Pesa proved to be a key multiplier for the product. Companies aiming to replicate Kenya's FinTech success should identify dormant or underused resources that can complement their innovations and foster growth.

CHAPTER 10
CHALLENGES AND OPPORTUNITIES FOR KENYA

HOWEVER, despite these challenges, Kenya has numerous opportunities that could transform its economic and social landscape. The country has a vast potential in technology, manufacturing, and renewable energy sectors. These sectors have the potential to create jobs, increase exports, and diversify the economy.

Kenya is also strategically located, with access to the Indian Ocean, making it an attractive destination for investment and trade. Additionally, the country has a young and educated workforce, which is critical in driving innovation and growth.

Kenya's devolved system of governance is another opportunity that could transform the country. This system has enabled the transfer of resources and decision-making to the county level, creating opportunities for local economic development and promoting social inclusion.

Regarding economic opportunities, Kenya has a rapidly growing technology sector, with innovative startups emerging and foreign investment pouring in. The country also has diverse natural resources, including fertile agricultural land, minerals, and offshore oil deposits. Additionally, Kenya has a large middle class, providing a growing consumer base and the potential for increased domestic consumption.

In conclusion, Kenya has unique challenges and opportunities as it continues to develop and grow globally. While significant hurdles exist, including political instability, corruption, and environmental degradation, there are also promising economic opportunities in technology, natural resources, and a growing middle class. Continued investment and support, both domestically and from the international community, will be crucial to address these challenges and help Kenya realize its full potential.

10.1 CHALLENGES FACING THE PEOPLE OF KENYA

The People of Kenya

Kenya is a diverse country with over 40 ethnic groups, each with its unique culture, language, and traditions. The country's population is estimated to be around 53 million, with the majority living in rural areas. Kenya's ethnic diversity is one of the country's defining features. There are over 60 languages spoken in Kenya, with English and Swahili being the official languages. Swahili is widely spoken across the country, and it is the language of trade and commerce. English is used in education, government, and business. The most widely spoken indigenous languages are Kikuyu, Luhya, Kalenjin, Luo, and Kamba.

Ethnic tensions and conflicts have led to violence in the past, particularly during elections. The government has tried to promote national unity and cohesion through initiatives such as the National Cohesion and Integration Commission. However, more must be done to address the root causes of ethnic tensions and conflicts.

Additionally, discrimination against minority ethnic groups, particularly the Somali and other Muslim communities, remains a challenge. The government has been accused of targeting these communities in the name of security, leading to human rights abuses and discrimination.

High level of corruption - This has become deeply entrenched in various government institutions. Corruption undermines economic growth and development by diverting resources that could be used to provide essential services and investments. It also creates an uneven playing field for businesses, hindering investment and economic growth.

Overreliance on a few key sectors - particularly agriculture and tourism. This dependence makes the country vulnerable to external shocks such as climate change, disease outbreaks, and global economic crises. It also limits the country's ability to diversify its economy and create job opportunities in other sectors.

Inadequate infrastructure, particularly in rural areas. This makes it difficult for businesses to operate, limiting their ability to expand and create jobs. It also limits access to essential services such as healthcare and education, hindering social development.

Poverty - Kenya is one of the poorest countries in the world, with a poverty rate of around 36%. Poverty is more prevalent in rural areas, where most of the population lives. The lack of access to basic services such as clean water, sanitation, and healthcare, coupled with limited job opportunities, perpetuates the cycle of poverty. The government and international organizations have implemented several poverty reduction programs, but more needs to be done to address the root causes of poverty.

Education - Kenya has made significant progress in improving access to education, with primary school enrolment rates increasing from 57% in 2003 to over 80% in 2018. However, access to quality education remains a challenge, particularly in rural areas. The quality of education is also affected by a shortage of teachers, inadequate infrastructure, and limited resources. The government has implemented several initiatives to improve the quality of education, including introducing free primary education and teacher training programs.

Healthcare - Access to healthcare is a significant challenge in Kenya, particularly in rural areas. The country has a shortage of health workers, inadequate infrastructure, and limited resources. The high prevalence of communicable diseases such as HIV/AIDS, malaria, and tuberculosis further strains the healthcare system. The government and international organizations have implemented several programs to improve access to healthcare, but more needs to be done to address the root causes of poor health outcomes.

Gender Equality - Gender inequality is a significant challenge in Kenya, with women and girls facing discrimination and limited opportunities in education, employment, and political participation. Women are also more vulnerable to gender-based violence, including domestic violence and sexual assault. The government and civil society organizations have made efforts to address gender inequality, including the adoption of the Gender Policy Framework and the enactment of laws to protect women's rights.

Kenya also faces environmental challenges, including deforestation, soil erosion, and desertification, which can lead to food insecurity and water scarcity.

Furthermore, Kenya is vulnerable to external economic shocks, such as fluctuations in commodity prices and changes in global trade policies. The COVID-19 pandemic has also significantly impacted the country's economy, highlighting the need for greater diversification and resilience.In conclusion, Kenya has enormous potential but faces significant challenges related to poverty, education, healthcare, gender inequality, and ethnic diversity. Addressing these challenges requires a comprehensive approach that involves the government, civil society organizations, and international partners. Despite the challenges, Kenya's people and natural resources provide a foundation for economic development and social progress. The next chapter will examine the country's economic potential and the challenges that must be addressed to realize it.

10.2 KENYA'S ENVIRONMENTAL CHALLENGES

Kenya is home to various natural environments, including savannah grasslands, tropical forests, and coastal ecosystems. However, over the past several decades, Kenya's environment has faced a number of challenges, ranging from deforestation and soil erosion to pollution and climate change. Kenya, like many other countries in Africa, faces a range of environmental challenges that have the potential to impact the country's economy, health, and social well-being. These challenges are the result of a combination of factors, including climate change, deforestation, overgrazing, and soil erosion.

Climate change -. The country has experienced various weather-related events in recent years, including droughts and floods, which have significantly impacted the country's agricultural sector and food security. In addition, rising temperatures and changing rainfall patterns are causing the spread of diseases such as malaria and dengue fever.

Deforestation -. The country's forests are being cleared at an alarming rate, primarily for the purposes of charcoal production and agriculture. This has led to biodiversity loss, soil erosion, and decreased water quality, among other negative impacts. The government has attempted to address this issue through initiatives such as the Forest Conservation and Management Act, but enforcement of these regulations remains a challenge.

Overgrazing -. Many areas of the country are used for livestock grazing, and overgrazing has lead to soil degradation, loss of vegetation, and decreased productivity. This is particularly problematic in areas where the land is already vulnerable due to drought and other environmental stressors.

Soil erosion -. The country's topography and heavy rainfall can lead to soil erosion, which can cause a range of negative impacts, including reduced soil fertility, decreased agricultural productivity, and increased water pollution. This is exacerbated by deforestation and poor land management practices.

Pollution -. Air pollution, caused by traffic and industrial emissions, is a growing problem in urban areas, leading to respiratory problems and other health issues. Water pollution is also a major concern, particularly in urban areas where industrial waste and untreated sewage are often dumped into rivers and lakes.

Degradation of its coastal ecosystems -. The country's long coastline is home to a diverse range of habitats, including mangroves, coral reefs, and seagrass beds. However, these ecosystems are under threat from a variety of factors, including overfishing, pollution, and climate change.

Overfishing is a major issue in Kenya's coastal waters, as local fishermen compete with commercial trawlers and foreign fishing fleets. This has led to declines in fish populations, which not only affects the livelihoods of local communities, but also has domino effects for the wider ecosystem.

Despite these challenges, Kenya has made significant progress in addressing environmental issues in recent years. For example, the government has launched initiatives aimed at reforestation and conservation, such as the Green Belt Movement and the Kenya Forest Service. In addition, the government has established marine protected areas and implemented regulations to limit fishing and reduce pollution. Civil society organizations and local communities are also involved in efforts to promote sustainable coastal development and conservation.

Kenya's culture and society are deeply interconnected with the natural world. Traditional practices such as farming, hunting, and fishing have long been shaped by the rhythms of the seasons and the availability of natural resources.

Today, many Kenyans are working to find ways to balance economic development and environmental protection, recognizing the importance for the country's future. Kenya has also become a leader in the development of renewable energy, particularly in the areas of wind and geothermal power. These initiatives help reduce greenhouse gas emissions and provide opportunities for job creation and economic development.

In conclusion, Kenya faces a range of environmental challenges that have the potential to impact the country's economy, health, and social well-being. These challenges are the result of a combination of factors, including climate change, deforestation, overgrazing, and soil erosion. Addressing these challenges will require a combination of government policies, public education, and private-sector engagement. Initiatives such as afforestation, sustainable land management practices, and climate adaptation strategies can help to mitigate these challenges and create a more sustainable future for Kenya. As an Africa expert, it is important to understand these challenges and advocate for policies and practices that can help address them.

10.3 THE SOLUTION TO KENYA'S ENVIRONMENTAL CHALLENGES

Kenya faces several environmental challenges, including climate change, deforestation, overgrazing, and soil erosion. These challenges significantly impact the country's economy, health, and social well-being. However, several solutions can be implemented to address these challenges.

Climate change -. To address this challenge, the country can focus on reducing greenhouse gas emissions through initiatives such as renewable energy development and energy efficiency measures. Kenya has already taken steps in this direction with the construction of the Lake Turkana Wind Power project, one of Africa's largest wind farms.

Promoting afforestation and reforestation -. The government can encourage tree-planting initiatives and incentivise landowners to participate. This will help to increase the country's forest cover, reduce soil erosion, and improve water quality.

Overgrazing -. to address this issue, the government can promote sustainable land management practices, such as rotational grazing, and support farmers to implement these practices. Additionally, promoting alternative protein sources, such as fish and poultry, can help reduce the demand for livestock and decrease the pressure on grazing lands.

Soil erosion -. To address this issue, the government can promote the use of sustainable land management practices, such as conservation tillage and cover cropping, to reduce soil erosion and improve soil health. Additionally, supporting small-scale farmers to implement these practices can help increase their adoption.

Finally, promoting public education and awareness is critical to addressing environmental challenges in Kenya. The government can develop public education campaigns to promote sustainable practices and raise awareness of the impacts of environmental degradation. Additionally, the government can engage with local communities and provide support to help them implement sustainable practices.

In conclusion, Kenya faces several environmental challenges, but several solutions can be implemented to address these challenges. These solutions include reducing greenhouse gas emissions, promoting afforestation and reforestation, promoting sustainable land management practices, and promoting public education and awareness. These initiatives will require a coordinated effort between the government, private sector, and civil society, but they can potentially create a more sustainable future for Kenya.

Global Financing Pact Summit in France

During the New Global Financing Pact, which took place on June 22, 2023, in Paris under the leadership of President Emmanuel Macron, leaders from the Global North and Global South came together to address the inequities in the global financial system. They aimed to empower developing nations to invest in clean energy and enhance their resilience against natural disasters.

Among the influential leaders at the summit, Kenya's President William Ruto made a notable impact with his presence and ideas. Ruto brought a fresh perspective to the discussions, advocating for a just energy transition. He emphasized that while wealthier nations must fulfil their commitments, African countries cannot afford to wait for action. Ruto highlighted Kenya's proactive approach and the country's potential to become a hub for carbon removal in the Rift Valley, emphasizing that climate solutions are not limited to the Global North but are also abundant in the Global South. He proudly shared that renewables already account for 92 percent of Kenya's electricity generation.

During the summit, Ruto made a significant breakthrough by seemingly endorsing the concept of Global Public Investment, which was pioneered in part by Jonathan Glennie in his book, "The Future of Aid." Ruto stressed the need for a new framework where everyone contributes, benefits, and collectively decides, focusing on utilizing public funds rather than relying solely on private resources.

At the Power Our Planet event, Ruto expressed frustration with narratives that portray Africans as passive victims of climate change, dependent on aid and grievances. Instead, he emphasized Africa's potential as an active participant in climate solutions, urging the continent to move beyond divisions and blame towards repairing trust and fostering a new type of solidarity based on fairness.

In tackling the climate crisis, Ruto stressed the importance of shared responsibility and envisioned a world where all nations contribute and pay based on their consumption. He advocated for a new multilateral climate change action mechanism funded by universal global carbon taxes on fossil fuels, aviation, marine transport, and other transactions to achieve this. This funding would support decarbonization, adaptation, and nature protection and regeneration. Ruto made it clear that Kenya is willing to contribute financially, stating, "We want to pay" during the summit's closing press conference.

In alignment with this objective, Kenya is actively participating in a taxation task force established during the summit. The task force's role is to explore and propose additional tax options, along with the maritime levy, and present a report on these initiatives at the upcoming Africa Climate Summit, which will be hosted in Nairobi later this year.

Ruto repeatedly emphasized that the issue at hand is not about a divide between the Global North and Global South or emitters versus non-emitters. It is about finding a win-win outcome. The statistics support Ruto's stance, as investing in a green global industrial revolution will benefit the entire world. The transition to a net-zero future holds significant potential for job creation, with a projected 14 million new jobs expected by 2030 in the clean energy sector. Following the net-zero pathway outlined by the International Energy Agency (IEA) would require a total annual energy investment of USD 5 trillion by 2030, contributing an additional 0.4 percentage point to annual global GDP growth. Despite the challenges posed by the Covid-19 pandemic and subsequent economic downturn in 2020, renewable energy sources experienced robust growth, while electric vehicles achieved record-breaking sales, demonstrating their resilience and sustained momentum.

President William Ruto captivated the audience with his global address in Paris, France, receiving enthusiastic cheers, claps, and admiration. As he spoke about climate change and financing to thousands of young scholars, each sentence uttered by the Head of State elicited warm applause and cheers, symbolizing the audience's support and affection. "I see the solutions and the future. It requires solidarity, strength, equity, and when I see you, I see a great future. We have the necessary technology. We have it in our power to make it right," Ruto declared, greeted by resounding cheers from the crowd. He emphasized that the event's primary objective is to advocate for a global financial system that is suitable for its purpose. "One that does not pit the West against the East, or the North against the South. We want one that is fair," he expressed passionately.

He extended an invitation to the youth to attend the Africa Climate Summit, scheduled to take place in Nairobi in September 2023.

10.4 THE FUTURE IS BRIGHT FOR THE PEOPLE OF KENYA

As the country strives for greater development and progress, the input and participation of its citizens are crucial. The people of Kenya have a responsibility to engage in the democratic process, hold their leaders accountable, and demand transparency and accountability in government.

One way in which the people of Kenya have shaped the country's future is by participating in elections and exercising their right to vote. This has allowed them to have a say in the country's direction and the policies implemented. Additionally, the people of Kenya can voice their concerns and opinions through peaceful protests, civil society organizations, and other forms of civic engagement.

Moreover, the people of Kenya can contribute to the country's development by actively participating in economic activities. This includes entrepreneurship, innovation, and job creation. By supporting local businesses, investing in education and skills training, and embracing technological advancements, the people of Kenya can contribute to the country's economic growth and prosperity.

Finally, the people of Kenya can also play a critical role in addressing the country's environmental challenges. This includes adopting sustainable practices, such as reforestation, conservation, and responsible use of natural resources. The people of Kenya can also advocate for environmentally sustainable development policies.

In conclusion, the people of Kenya are essential in shaping the country's future. Their participation in the democratic process, economic activities, and environmental conservation will determine the direction and progress of the country. As such, it is essential to empower and engage the people of Kenya in the development process and ensure their voices are heard and their contributions are valued.

10.5 THE SIGNIFICANCE OF KENYA WITHIN AFRICA AND THE WORLD

Kenya occupies a critical place in the African continent and the world at large. With a population of over 50 million people, Kenya is the largest economy in East Africa and a key player in the region's politics and diplomacy. Kenya's strategic location at the crossroads of East Africa makes it a hub for trade and commerce, with the country serving as a gateway to the wider African market.

Kenya's importance to the world is not limited to its strategic location and economic potential. The country has also played a key role in regional peacekeeping and conflict resolution efforts, helping to stabilize neighbouring countries such as Somalia and South Sudan. Kenya has also been a key player in promoting regional integration and economic cooperation in East Africa, with initiatives such as the East African Community (EAC) and the African Continental Free Trade Area (AfCFTA).

Furthermore, Kenya has been at the forefront of global efforts to tackle pressing challenges such as climate change and poverty. The country has committed to reducing its carbon emissions and investing in renewable energy while implementing poverty reduction programs and promoting inclusive economic growth.

Kenya's contributions to art, literature, and music are also significant. The country's rich cultural heritage and artistic expressions have helped to shape the wider African identity and cultural landscape.

Kenya's significance within Africa and the world is also reflected in its diplomatic relations with other countries. Kenya has a strong presence in the international community, with active participation in multilateral organizations such as the United Nations (UN), the World Trade Organization (WTO), and the African Union (AU).

Kenya's diplomatic relations with other countries have also helped to strengthen its position in the region and the world. The country has established close ties with its East African neighbours and major powers such as China, the United States, and the European Union. These relationships have helped to foster greater economic cooperation and promote regional stability.

Moreover, Kenya's contributions to global development and humanitarian efforts have been significant. The country has received aid and support from various international organizations but has also been a donor and contributor to development programs in other African countries. Kenya has been a leader in promoting health and education initiatives in the region, with programs such as the United Nations Children's Fund (UNICEF) and the Global Partnership for Education.

Kenya's role in the global arena is shaped by several factors, including its strategic location, political stability, and economic potential. As a result, the country has become a key player in regional politics, particularly in the East African Community (EAC) and the African Union (AU). Additionally, Kenya has contributed to international peacekeeping efforts, particularly in Somalia, where it has deployed troops as part of the African Union Mission in Somalia (AMISOM).

In the economic realm, Kenya is the largest economy in East Africa and has significant potential for growth. The country has a vibrant private sector, particularly in the technology industry, and is home to several multinational corporations. Additionally, Kenya has significant natural resources, including oil, gas, and minerals, which could help to drive economic growth.

Kenya needs to focus on several key areas to further achieve its role in the global arena. First, the country must continue promoting political stability and good governance. This includes addressing corruption and ensuring that elections are free and fair. Additionally, Kenya needs to continue to play a leading role in regional politics, particularly in the EAC and the AU. This includes promoting regional integration and economic cooperation.

Secondly, Kenya must focus on economic development and promote investment in key sectors, such as infrastructure, agriculture, and technology. This includes developing policies to attract foreign investment, improving the business environment, and promoting innovation and entrepreneurship. Additionally, the country needs to focus on sustainably developing its natural resources, ensuring they benefit the people of Kenya and promote economic growth.

Thirdly, Kenya needs to continue to play a leading role in international peacekeeping efforts. This includes providing troops for peacekeeping missions, promoting dialogue and reconciliation in conflict zones, and supporting efforts to prevent conflict and promote stability.

Fourthly, Kenya needs to prioritize environmental sustainability and address climate change. This includes promoting renewable energy development, reducing greenhouse gas emissions, and addressing deforestation and soil erosion. Additionally, the country needs to promote sustainable land management practices and improve water management.

Fifthly, Kenya needs to focus on promoting education and human development. This includes improving access to education and healthcare, promoting gender equality, and supporting marginalized communities.

Kenya also needs to prioritize collaboration and partnership with other countries and international organizations. This includes working with regional partners such as Tanzania, Uganda, and Rwanda and international partners such as the United States, China, and the European Union. Additionally, Kenya must engage with international organizations such as the United Nations and the World Bank to access financing and technical support.

Finally, Kenya's role becomes even more critical as the world faces new and emerging challenges such as the COVID-19 pandemic. The country has demonstrated resilience and innovation in responding to the pandemic, from implementing digital solutions to producing essential medical supplies. This crisis has highlighted the need for greater international cooperation and solidarity, and Kenya can play a crucial role in promoting this.

In conclusion, Kenya plays a significant role in the global arena and has the potential to become an even more influential player in the future. To achieve this, the country must focus on political stability, economic development, international peacekeeping efforts, environmental sustainability, and human development. Additionally, Kenya needs to prioritize collaboration and partnership with other countries and international organizations. By pursuing these goals, Kenya can become a model for other countries in Africa and beyond and help to promote peace, stability, and prosperity in the region and the world.

10.6 THE NEED FOR CONTINUED INVESTMENT AND SUPPORT IN KENYA'S DEVELOPMENT

Kenya has made significant strides in various sectors over the years, but the country still faces numerous challenges that threaten to hinder its development. Therefore, there is a need for continued investment and support in Kenya's development to address these challenges and unlock its potential fully.

One of the critical areas that require investment and support is infrastructure. Kenya has made progress in expanding its infrastructure, but there is still a significant deficit in areas such as roads, energy, and water supply. The lack of adequate infrastructure hinders economic growth and development, making attracting investments and creating job opportunities challenging. Therefore, continued investment in infrastructure development is critical to unlock Kenya's economic potential.

Another critical area that requires investment is education. Despite the government's efforts to improve access to education, many children still do not have access to quality education, particularly in rural areas. This limits their ability to reach their full potential and participate fully in Kenya's development. Therefore, investment in education is critical to provide the necessary skills and knowledge to support Kenya's economic growth and development.

Investment in technology and innovation is also critical in Kenya's development. Kenya has already demonstrated its potential as a leader in technology and innovation with the success of initiatives such as M-Pesa. Therefore, continued investment in this sector can provide opportunities for growth and development, particularly for small and medium enterprises.

Finally, continued support in Kenya's development is critical in addressing social challenges such as poverty, inequality, and unemployment. The government has made efforts to address these challenges, but continued support is necessary to achieve sustainable development and ensure that no one is left behind.

In conclusion, continued investment and support in Kenya's development are critical to fully address the country's challenges and unlock its potential. Investment in infrastructure, education, technology, and innovation and addressing social challenges will enable Kenya to achieve sustainable development and contribute to the advancement of Africa and the world. Therefore, international partners need to continue supporting Kenya's development agenda to create a more prosperous, equitable, and sustainable future for all.

CONCLUSION

Kenya's history is a complex and multifaceted story that spans thousands of years, from the earliest human settlements in East Africa to the present day. This book has attempted to provide a comprehensive overview of the country's rich cultural heritage, its struggles against colonialism and oppression, and its ongoing efforts to build a stable and prosperous nation.

Kenya's journey to independence was marked by years of resistance and sacrifice, with leaders like Jomo Kenyatta and Dedan Kimathi playing key roles in the fight for freedom. However, the post-independence period was challenging, with political instability, corruption, and ethnic tensions hindering the country's progress.

Kenya has made significant strides in economic development, technology, and innovation in recent years. However, the country continues to face challenges such as climate change, environmental degradation, and insecurity. Addressing these challenges will require sustained effort and cooperation from both domestic and international actors.

Ultimately, Kenya's future is in the hands of its people, who have shown time and again their resilience and determination in the face of adversity. As the country looks towards the future, it will be important to build on its strengths, address its weaknesses, and work towards a more just, equitable, and prosperous society.

The world needs Kenya for many reasons, including its role as a regional hub for trade, innovation, and development. Kenya's strategic location makes it an important gateway to East and Central Africa, with its ports and transport infrastructure serving as key links between landlocked countries and global markets.

Moreover, Kenya has a rich cultural heritage and a diverse society that has much to offer to the world regarding art, music, literature, and other forms of creative expression. The country's people are known for their resilience and entrepreneurial spirit, which has helped to drive economic growth and development in recent years.

However, Kenya also faces significant challenges, including poverty, inequality, and environmental degradation. Addressing these challenges will require sustained effort, commitment from the government and civil society, and support from international partners and donors.

In conclusion, Kenya is a country with a rich history and a bright future. Its people have shown remarkable resilience and determination in the face of adversity and have made significant strides in areas such as economic development, technology, and innovation. However, the country also faces significant challenges that must be addressed if it is to fully realize its potential. By working together, Kenya and its partners can build a more just, equitable, and prosperous future for all.

REFERENCES

1. African Development Bank Group. (2021). Kenya Country Brief. African Development Bank Group.
2. Edgerton, R. E. (1991). Mau Mau: An African Crucible. New York: Ballantine Books, p.6.
3. Furedi, F. (1989). The Mau Mau War in Perspective. London: James Currey Ltd, p.114
4. Gatheru, R. M. (2005). Kenya: From Colonisation to Independence, 1888-1970. Jefferson: McFarland & Company, p.144.
5. Furedi, F. (1989). The Mau Mau War in Perspective. London: James Currey Ltd, p
6. Fenton, N., & German, L. (2018). Governance, devolution, and local development in Kenya. Journal of Eastern African Studies, 12(3), 488-505.
7. Gatheru, R. M. (2005). Kenya: From Colonisation to Independence, 1888-1970. Jefferson: McFarland & Company.
8. Gitonga, Z. K. (2019). The Impact of Technological Innovation on Economic Development in Kenya. Journal of Economics and Sustainable Development, 10(6), 62-76.

9. Hodd, M. (2012). East African Handbook. Footprint Handbooks.

10. Kennedy, D. (1992). 'Constructing the Colonial Myth of Mau Mau' The International Journal of African Historical Studies 25, pp.241-260.

11. Kenya National Bureau of Statistics. (2021). Economic Survey 2021. Government of Kenya.

12. Mambo, E. H. (2005). The Kenya Land and Freedom Army: A Select Annotated Bibliography. Africa World Press.

13. Munene, I. I. (2018). The Challenges of Achieving Sustainable Development in Kenya: An Analysis of the 2030 Agenda. Journal of Sustainable Development, 11(6), 83-97.

14. Mwaura, S. (2019). Kenya's Foreign Policy: A Critical Analysis. Africa Institute of South Africa.

15. Ndung'u, N. S. (2017). Challenges and opportunities of devolution in Kenya. Journal of Public Administration and Governance, 7(4), 137-153.

16. Ochieng, W. R. (1990). Themes in Kenyan History. Nairobi: Heinemann Kenya Limited.

17. Odhiambo, M. O. (2015). History of Kenya. Palgrave Macmillan.

18. Ogot, B. A. (1995). Kenya: From Pre-colonial to Post-colonial Times. East African Educational Publishers.

19. Oyugi, W. O. (2008). Kenya: The Struggle for Democracy. Zed Books.

20. Republic of Kenya. (2010). Constitution of Kenya. Government of Kenya.

21. Tignor, R. L. (1976). The Colonial Transformation of Kenya. Princeton: Princeton University Press.

22. UNDP. (2020). Human Development Report 2020: The Next Frontier - Human Development and the Anthropocene.

23. United Nations Development Programme. United Nations Environment Programme. (2021). Kenya: Environmental Snapshot. United Nations Environment Programme.
24. United Nations Development Programme. (2019). Human Development Indices and Indicators: 2019 Statistical Update. United Nations Development Programme.
25. Wa-Githumo, Mwangi. (1991). 'The Truth about the Mau Mau Movement: The Most Popular Uprising in Kenya' Transafrican Journal of History 20, pp.1-18
26. Wa-Githumo, Mwangi. (1991). 'The Truth about the Mau Mau Movement: The Most Popular Uprising in Kenya' Transafrican Journal of History 20, p.9. ?
27. World Bank. (2021). Kenya. World Bank Group.

GLOSSARY

1. Anthropocene - a proposed geological epoch characterized by significant human impact on the Earth's ecosystems and geology.
2. Big Four Agenda - a set of development priorities established by the Kenyan government, including affordable housing, universal healthcare, food security, and manufacturing.
3. Brain drain - the emigration of highly skilled or educated individuals from their home country to seek better opportunities elsewhere.
4. Brain gain - the reverse migration of highly skilled or educated individuals back to their home country, often contributing to social and economic development.
5. Child labour - the use of children in work that is harmful to their health, safety, or development, often associated with poverty and lack of education.
6. Climate change - the long-term alteration of global weather patterns and ecosystems caused by human activity, including the burning of fossil fuels and deforestation.

7. Corruption - the abuse of power for personal gain, often involving bribery or embezzlement of public funds.
8. Devolution - the transfer of power and decision-making from a central government to local or regional authorities.
9. Diaspora - a group of people who live outside of their ancestral homeland, often referring to those who have migrated from Africa to other parts of the world.
10. Digital divide - the gap between those with access to modern information and communication technologies and those without, often related to economic and social inequalities.
11. Ethnocentrism is the belief in the superiority of one's ethnic or cultural group, often resulting in prejudice and discrimination against others.
12. FGM - female genital mutilation, a harmful practice involving the partial or total removal of female genitalia, often associated with cultural traditions and beliefs.
13. Gender inequality - the unequal treatment and opportunities for individuals based on their gender, often resulting in social, economic, and political disparities.
14. Globalization - the process of increasing interconnectedness and interdependence among countries, economies, and cultures around the world.
15. HIV/AIDS - a viral disease that attacks the immune system and has significantly impacted public health and social issues in Kenya and many other countries.
16. Human rights - the fundamental rights and freedoms all human beings are entitled to, often protected by international laws and conventions.
17. Harambee - a tradition in Kenya of community self-help events, such as fundraising or volunteer work.
18. Informal economy - economic activities that are not regulated or taxed by the government and are often carried out by individuals or small businesses.

19. Maasai - a pastoralist ethnic group in Kenya and Tanzania known for its distinctive customs and dress.
20. Matatu - a type of public transportation in Kenya, often consisting of minibuses or vans.
21. Mau Mau - a Kenyan nationalist and rebel movement that fought against British colonial rule in the 1950s.
22. Neocolonialism - a form of indirect colonialism in which developed countries maintain economic and political influence over developing countries.
23. Refugee crisis - a global humanitarian crisis involving the displacement of millions of people from their homes due to war, conflict, and persecution.
24. Sustainable development - development that meets the needs of the present without compromising the ability of future generations to meet their own needs.
25. Swahili - a Bantu language spoken in many countries in East Africa, including Kenya, Tanzania, and Uganda.
26. Trade liberalization - the removal of barriers to international trade, such as tariffs and quotas, often aimed at promoting economic growth and development.
27. Traditional medicine - alternative healthcare practices that are often rooted in cultural or spiritual beliefs and are widely used in Kenya and other parts of the world.
28. UN Sustainable Development Goals - a set of 17 goals adopted by the United Nations in 2015, aimed at ending poverty, protecting the planet, and promoting prosperity for all.
29. Urbanization - the process of increasing population and development in urban areas, often resulting in social, economic, and environmental challenges.
30. Wildlife conservation - the protection and preservation of wild animals and their habitats.